√KRAMER, Jack. *Natural Dyes: Plants & Processes.* drawings by Charles Hoeppner. 144p. photogs., some color. index. Scribners. 1972. $9.95. ISBN 0-684-12828-4. LC 76-179554. CRAFTS

This book, like Alma Lesch's *Vegetable Dyeing* (LJ, June 1, 1971) and Rita Adrosko's *Natural Dyes & Home Dyeing* (Dover, 1971. pap.) offers color recipes, detailed instructions on the use of mordants and preparation of plant parts, and fibers to be dyed. There are superb drawings of plants. Kramer is an experimenter, and he urges readers to experiment. The Adrosko was originally published as United States National Museum Bulletin 281 by the Smithsonian Institution Press and thus has the authority of the museum behind it; about one-third of the book is "historical background" and excerpts from early books. Lesch is a professional, an instructor and consultant on textiles, yarns, & dyeing, and her book is good for the serious, experienced dyer. These three books complement each other; Kramer is for the novice and general reader. It meets the needs of the school or small public library.—*Bertha K. Wilson, formerly Chief Librarian, Veterans Administration, Downey, Ill.*

This is an uncorrected proof of a review scheduled for Library Journal, Mar. 1, 1973

Natural
Dyes
plants
&processes

Natural
Dyes
plants
&processes

by Jack Kramer

DRAWINGS BY CHARLES HOEPPNER

Charles Scribner's Sons
New York

Books by Jack Kramer

WATER GARDENING
MINIATURE PLANTS INDOORS AND OUT
GARDEN PLANNING FOR THE SMALL PROPERTY
HANGING GARDENS
GARDENING WITH STONE AND SAND
THE NATURAL WAY TO PEST-FREE GARDENING
FERNS AND PALMS FOR INTERIOR DECORATION
NATURAL DYES: PLANTS AND PROCESSES

Acknowledgments

In the course of writing this book, many fine people, friends and strangers alike, have come to my aid. I am especially indebted to Mary Martinez, who first introduced me to natural plant dyeing and who in the ensuing months offered her enthusiasm and help.

To the following craftsmen in the Mill Valley area I owe special thanks: Charlene Jackson, who contributed finished pieces of natural-dyed yarns; and Liz Douglas, who volunteered recipes for dyes. A special vote of thanks goes to Pam Kleyman of San Francisco, who let me use the sample yarn book of her own recipes to fashion my yarn color chart.

At various art and craft shows throughout Marin County, and especially the Art and Craft Show of Mill Valley, I met many fine craftsmen who discussed freely with me the art of natural dyeing with plants and showed me their finished wares. To them I owe a special debt of gratitude.

Once again, to my artist, Charles Hoeppner, who contributed the fine drawings for this book, I give my appreciation; and to Judy Smith, who gave up her weekends for many months to type this manuscript, I say thanks again.

Contents

ACKNOWLEDGMENTS   7

AUTHOR'S NOTE   15

INTRODUCTION: A Treasure House of Color   19

1

The Natural Beauty of Color   *21*

PLANT MATERIALS   *22*
WHEN TO GATHER PLANTS   *24*
THE WORK SPACE   *24*

2

Preparing and Washing Wool; Mordanting   *26*

PREPARING YARNS   *28*
WASHING YARNS   *30*
MORDANTING WOOL   *32*
Alum (aluminum potassium sulfate)   *34*
Chrome (potassium dichromate)   *36*
Copper sulfate (blue vitriol)   *36*
Tin (stannous chloride)   *38*
Iron (ferrous sulfate)   *39*

HOW TO MORDANT OTHER FIBERS
Cotton and Linen   40
Cotton and Linen (2nd method)   40
Silk   41
MORDANTING WITH AND AFTER
THE DYE   42

3

Getting the Dye Material 43

FLOWERS, LEAVES, AND BERRIES   44
BARKS, ROOTS, AND HULLS   47
LIST OF TREES   *50*
GRASSES AND WEEDS   *55*
STEMS, TWIGS, AND VINES   *55*
HOUSEHOLD ITEMS   *56*
LICHENS   *56*

4

The Dyeing Process 60

BLOOMING AND SADDENING WOOL   *62*
NOTES ON DYED COLORS   *63*
COLORFASTNESS   *64*
TOP-DYEING   *65*

5

Commercial Woods,
Prepared Plant Materials 66

MADDER   67
Recipe for Red   67
Recipe for Orange   69
LOGWOOD   70
Recipe for Violet   70
FUSTIC   70
Recipe for Bright Yellow   71
INDIGO   72
Stock Solution for Indigo   72
CUTCH   74
Recipe for Rich Brown   74
COCHINEAL   75
Recipe for American Beauty Red   75
Recipe for Magenta   75
Recipe for Bright Orange   76

6

Color 77

SOME COLOR BASICS   79
SOME COLOR COMBINATIONS   80
USING COLOR IN COMPOSITIONS   81

7
Dyer's Garden 83

PERENNIALS AND ANNUALS   84
List of Perennial and Annual Flowers   85
SOWING SEED   92
Seed Mixes   94
The Seed-Sown Garden   97
SHRUBS   101
How to Plant Shrubs   102
List of Shrubs   102

8
Dye Recipes 114

NOTES ON RECIPES   *115*
RECIPES:
Acacia Pods   *115*
Blackberry Shoots (saddened)   Black Walnut Hulls   116
Black Walnut Leaves   Bougainvillea   117
Coffee   Dock   Eucalyptus Bark   118
Fennel   Flowering Plum Leaves   119
Golden Poppy   Heather   Horsetail   120
Lichen (yellow)   Lichen with Indigo Overdye
    Logwood Chips   122
Lombardy Poplar Leaves   Lupine Flowers (purple)   123

Privet Berries   Privet Leaves   Red Onion Skins   124
Rhododendron Leaves   Stag's Horn Moss   125
Sage   Silver Dollar Eucalyptus (tin bloomed)   126
Yellow Onion Skins   127
Color Charts   128

APPENDIX   *137*

INFORMATION ON SUPPLIES   *137*

SOURCES FOR PLANTS   *139*

BOOKS OF INTEREST   *140*

INDEX   *141*

Author's Note

I first saw natural-dyed materials about three years ago when a local weaver showed me some yarns. One color was derived from blueberry shoots, another from grape leaves. He told me (because I was a garden writer) what processes he had gone through to extract natural color from the plants. At that time I thought it was a lot of work to do when commercial dyes were so easy to use. I was not intrigued but I was interested, and what I had seen stayed lodged in my mind. In the ensuing months I learned that several craftsman in the area were starting to dye their materials with plants. This furthered my curiosity and I did some research. I was still interested, but not sufficiently motivated to write a book on the subject.

During some leisure weekends that followed, upon the insistence of a weaver, Mary Martinez, I was prompted into dyeing some yarns for the heck of it. We did get a lovely green color from poplar leaves and fine golds from onion skins, but still I was just interested. Then, one day at a local art show, I saw a small wall hanging, a weaving. It caught my eye immediately. There was something different about it that made it special. I compared it with the other hangings at the show. The pattern was not that outstanding, nor the weaving technique that good, but something was different, and as I looked at it again I knew. It was the colors. On further investigation I found it to be made exclusively of natural-dyed yarns.

What followed was more weekends of feverish dye experimentation in my kitchen. Plants had always been my excitement, and here was a new (really ancient) role for them. Just what dye colors would I get from chrysanthemums or dahlias? I gave my dyed yarns to various craftsmen in the area and their finished products were photographed for this book.

Now, of course, dyeing plants to color yarns is enjoying a renaissance. I no longer wonder what makes people spend their time going through the various processes. I know. The pages that follow contain this information. It is yet another way (and an immensely satisfying way to a garden writer) in which plants contribute to our world. In these natural-dyed yarns we see nature at her best enriching our lives for years to come.

Jack Kramer
Mill Valley
California

Natural
Dyes
plants
&processes

Natural-dyed yarns possess distinctive colors, unmatched by commercial dyes. *(Photo by Joyce R. Wilson)*

Introduction:
A Treasure House
of Color

Dyeing materials with plants is not new; it is an ancient art, inexpensive, easy to do, and gives you an affinity with nature. Dye plants were used in Greek and Roman times, and the medieval monks also used natural dyes for their garments.

When aniline dyes were introduced, about a century ago, exact colors became commercially available, mass production started, and the art of dyeing with plants was forgotten. It is only recently that we have discovered the beauty and fascination of this ancient craft. While it is true that this method is more trouble than using commercial packet dyes, no chemical-dyed yarn has the richness of color, the soft light and shadows, that natural-dyed yarns give to fabrics. This is because the color is alive as nature is alive.

The art of dyeing plants for coloring material—wool, cotton, linen, or silk—is a combination of plant and nature, craft and you. You do not have to be a botanist or artist to enjoy it.

This book includes many recipes involving different dye plants, but these are not the only plants to use. Half the fun is experimenting to see what different plants will yield in the dye pot. And no matter where you live, nature's materials are there for you to try.

With this book, a whole new world of color is at your finger-tips. You will see ancient weavings and tapestries in a new light. Colors you have never seen before, colors that are not available commercially, wait for you in nature.

For the craftsman these are *the beautiful colors*. All you need to unlock this treasure house of color is this book, some plants, a kitchen, and a love of nature.

1
The Natural Beauty of Color

Nature is special, and so are her colors. Part of the fun of dyeing yarn with natural color is picking blossoms from your yard or gathering leaves from meadows and forests to see what you can get. Once you start working with nature, you will appreciate flowers and plants not only for their beauty but for the colors they may yield in the dye pot. (Even weeds are storehouses of color!) Whether you are a weaver or an embroiderer, making apparel, rugs, or tapestries, there is an infinite choice of unmatched colors in everyday plants, and only you can bring the colors forth by the magic of the dye pot.

Using plants for dyeing yarns is similar to gourmet cooking. A combination of things is involved in each recipe: ingredients, timing, measurement, boiling, and simmering. Like food recipes, no two dye recipes are the same. Fresh flowers produce one color, dried flowers produce another. For example, young green leaves picked in spring yield a different color from mature leaves gathered in fall. Climate, rain, and soil also influence the colors inherent in plants: in Vermont you can get a violet color from dandelion roots, but not in California; in the West the weed imparts yellow to yarns. It is the uncertainty that makes this craft a unique adventure, and the colors produced are truly distinctive.

Wool is the favorite dyeing material. Cotton and linen are more difficult to work with, and should be approached only after you have mastered the dyeing technique with wool.

You might want to spin your own wool or buy it in skeins at yarn shops. Buy unbleached wool; it ranges in color from white to beige. Whether spun by hand or at a factory, wool has a certain amount of oil in it, and it is necessary to remove this oil before mordanting or dyeing (a mordant is a substance used to bind the color to the fiber. It is explained in the next chapter) or the wool won't absorb color. Bleached fibers can occasionally be used, too, but they do not dye as well as the natural kind.

Yarn is available by skein or by pound; buy enough at one time to complete the object you want to make. A second purchase of yarn may be of a slightly different color, and the dye may be a slightly different color as well.

PLANT MATERIALS

There are many natural plant materials for dyeing yarns: roots, barks, leaves, berries, seeds, twigs, branches, tubers, and nut hulls. Depending upon the recipe, the plant is either crushed (stems and roots) or used as is (leaves and flowers). Some plant parts are used fresh; others can be used dried. Woods not available in this country, such as madder, indigo, logwood, and fustic, can be purchased at botanical supply houses or yarn shops. They are available in chips or as extracts in powdered form (see Chapter 5).

As mentioned, the dye color varies with the type of plant, when it is gathered, and where it grows, and furthermore, the color depends on the amount gathered and the kind of mordant used.

A whole palette of color is available to the dyer. Gray shades come from blackberry twigs and leaves, or from butternut hulls. You can get shades of yellow from poplar leaves, onion skins, and dahlias. Dark browns and tans come from tree barks, and lily of the valley leaves yield a lime color. Yellows and gold are prevalent in plant material and can be obtained from goldenrod, privet, smartweed, and marguerites, for example.

Your garden can furnish a great many plants for dye work. Indeed, a garden may be the only sure way to secure enough plant material at one time to make a dye bath, since the same flowers picked three weeks later may yield a different color.

To determine how much plant material you need for dyeing, use twice as many twigs, leaves, stems, etc. (by volume) as yarn. For example, if you are dyeing one pound of yarn you will need at least two to three pounds of fresh plant material. For collecting we use the large paper grocery bags marked "one-sixth barrel size."

Tree barks make good dyes, and although I do not suggest stripping trees, some trees like birch and eucalyptus shed bark naturally. With other trees, take the bark from the limbs but not from the trunk so you will not harm the tree; collect the bark in spring when the sap is running. Because all barks contain tannic acid, which has brown coloring matter, you will get lively shades of brown and black in the dye bath. Trees whose barks yield colorful dyes include ash, birch, walnut, and alder.

Lichens are another source of dye, and grow in woodsy areas on tree trunks and rocks. These beautiful fungus formations can be found in spring or in summer; soak them overnight in water before you boil them for dye. Although lichens do not need a mordant, most of the colors they produce are fugitive and subject to fading.

WHEN TO GATHER PLANTS

Various plants, roots, or flowers may be picked at different times of the year. The colors they yield depend on the weather of the past season and the present season. If there has been little sun or if the summer has been unusually dry, the colors will not be strong.

Where a plant grows—soil and climate—is another factor that determines its color in the dye bath. In one region the plant may have a dark rich color; in a different place the same plant may produce a less colorful dye.

Lichen growing on rocks will yield a different color from the same lichen growing on trees, and the dye from tree bark varies, too, depending on whether you collect the outer or inner bark.

Even the time of day the material is gathered can sometimes influence the color the plant will give.

THE WORK SPACE

Years ago, mordanting and dyeing were generally outdoor projects, but today they can be easily done in the kitchen. Some members of the family may object to the occasionally unpleasant cooking odors of plant materials, but when they see the lovely colors the dyed yarns become they will probably be in the kitchen with you trying to see how this magic takes place. However, during the dye process do keep the stove ventilating fan going.

The most important pieces of equipment are suitable pots for the mordanting and dyeing process. Use enamel or glass vessels. I prefer the old-fashioned enamel ten-quart canners—which, by the way, are now available again in good hardware stores, although they are more costly than they were twenty years ago. You also need glass measures—pints, quarts, gallons—measuring spoons, and a glass funnel. For stirring and lifting the yarn skeins from the water, glass rods are perfect because wooden ones stain. A pestle and mortar are handy for crushing and grinding plant parts, and a chopping board and sharp knife are ideal for cutting plants.

The mordants such as chrome, tin, iron, generally come in small glass bottles, or metal containers for alum. Be sure to keep the mordants, in their proper containers, on high shelves out of the reach of children or pets, because some mordants are poisonous.

A standard kitchen range is fine for heating liquids. A gas flame is preferable because gradual heating, as opposed to the sudden heat changes so common with electric stoves, is needed in almost all processes.

A few dishpans are a necessity, too, so that you can rinse yarns easily; a scale that weighs in fractions of an ounce and some cheesecloth for straining the dye liquid are other requirements.

In a drawer keep labels, scissors, a notebook, and a pencil. Be sure to make accurate notes of the dye produced. Mark down exact amounts of mordants and kinds and amounts of plants in case you want to try to duplicate the dye.

Below the drawer have a shelf for keeping plant parts with plastic bags or gallon jars, and rubber gloves you can wear to avoid staining your hands.

2
Preparing and Washing Wool; Mordanting

Natural dyeing of raw yarn with plant materials is basically done in three steps: washing, mordanting, and dyeing. Each process depends on the other, and even though some yarns can be dyed without mordants, the majority require them.

The word *mordant* means to bite or to be caustic; in dyeing it refers to the chemical or substance used to fix the color to the yarn. During mordanting a chemical symbiosis occurs, and the metallic oxides and salts from the mordants become dissolved and fixed into the fibers, making the dye permanent or fast against washing and light. Through the years mordanted wool may fade somewhat, but colors remain beautiful.

Indigo is a versatile dye; in this shawl the color ranges from light blue to dark blue. The brown dye is black walnut leaves without a mordant. The shawl has shown no fading of color after six months; on the contrary, it has become richer in hue. *(Photo by author)*

The nonmordant dyes (those that are fairly fast without additional chemicals) give their color directly to wool without any preliminary steps. Lichens and gall nuts (already containing tannin) are typical plants that supply nonmordant dyes.

Generally, mordanting *precedes* the dyeing of the wool, but it can also be done *in conjunction with* the dyeing (put in the same pot), or it may be done *after* the dyeing process. The first method is the best for the beginner and generally produces brighter colors.

PREPARING YARNS

Yarns not in skeins are almost impossible to handle properly. But you can wind yarn easily; use a yarn winder or make skeins by wrapping the yarn around the legs of an upside-down chair. Two wooden dowels about ten inches high and twenty-four inches apart are another device that facilitates winding the yarn. But to me, the old-fashioned way is the fastest and easiest: bend your arm and wind the yarn around your hand and elbow. When the skeins are finished (half or one-pound weight), tie the skeins loosely with string in three or four places.

As mentioned, most wool, whether hand spun or machine spun, has a certain amount of oil that must be removed before mordanting or dyeing. Washing the wool is absolutely necessary for even coloring. Otherwise, solutions will not penetrate the materials; how thoroughly you wash the wool will also affect the color it takes from the dye bath.

Many craftsmen prefer to spin their own yarn, but home-spun yarn does not take color as readily as factory yarn; the dye color is not as bright.

Unbleached yarns for dyeing *Photo by Joyce R. Wilson*

WASHING YARNS

All fibers should be weighed dry and thoroughly cleaned before they are mordanted. There are several ways to wash wool, but the basic method is to wash and then to gently squeeze out suds and keep rinsing until the water runs clear. Wash the yarn in warm water (100°F.) with 3 to 4 ounces of neutral soap (Ivory Flakes are ideal) to 5 gallons of water for each pound of wool. Be sure that the water covers the yarn. Rinse in water of the same temperature three or four times until all soap has been eliminated. (You can add a little vinegar to the final rinse to completely cleanse the yarn of soap.) Some craftsmen simmer the wool in the pot for about 30 minutes, but this procedure makes the wool somewhat sticky.

Soft water is essential to the washing because the alkalinity of hard water can attack wool fibers and prevent the dye from forming a perfect solution. Add a small amount of a water softener such as Calgon to your kitchen water if it is hard, or you can make a fairly good water softener by dissolving 1 pound of washing soda (sal soda) in 1 quart of water.

Avoid shrinkage by handling the wool quickly and gently, always squeezing excess moisture from the material. Never wring or twist wool. Avoid sudden temperature changes in the water, or the wool will shrink and become harsh. Keep the temperature of the material as even as possible by transferring yarns directly from suds to rinse.

When washing cotton or linen, dissolve a neutral soap in water of 140°F. (Use about 5 gallons of water.) Wash the material thoroughly, and rinse it repeatedly to get rid of all the soap. Allow the material to soak in the final rinse for 30 minutes, then rinse it again. If you boil materials for about 1 hour to make sure they are thoroughly clean, rinse them afterwards.

Weighing dry yarn

Washing yarn *Photos by Joyce R. Wilson*

MORDANTING WOOL

There are several chemicals that can be used as mordants, but the best ones for the beginner are alum, chrome, tin, copper, and iron, all available from suppliers. Each mordant and the quantity used will affect the color of the yarn when it is dyed. The metallic salts produce colors inherent in the kind of metal from which the chemical is made. Thus iron gives a purple color or green or black tones, chrome enhances shades of brass or gold, and tin brightens colors.

Wool and silk are animal fibers, and because of their content can hold chemical oxides so that dyestuffs can combine with fabrics for permanent color. Cotton and other vegetable fibers—linen and raffia—do not absorb metallic mordants easily. However, they do combine with tannic acid, which is a natural constituent of oak galls, sumac leaves, and many tree barks. Tannic acid is thus then used either as a mordant or as an agent for fixing the mordant to the fiber.

To start the mordanting, have water ready, an enamel or glass pot, and the chemical agent. Be sure the pot is large enough to accommodate the yarn skeins; if crowded, they become felted.

As the wool cooks, replace evaporated water with enough water to keep the original recipe proportions. Each mordant has its own directions, but with all of them it is important not to let the water boil. It must simmer like soup, with no sudden temperature changes. Keep the yarn submerged in the pot. Stir wool occasionally.

Alum. Of the many different types of alum, aluminum potassium sulphate is the kind most commonly used in vegetable dyeing. Alum comes in granules or powdered form; a pound is inexpensive and

Equipment for mordanting *Photo by Joyce R. Wilson*

Different mordants *Photos by Joyce R. Wilson*

will mordant about 5 pounds of wool. Do not use too much alum or the wool will get sticky and gummy; you will have to experiment. (Our recipe calls for 3 to 4 ounces per pound of wool.) Since household cream of tartar distributes the mordant evenly through the yarn, it is usually added to most recipes.

ALUM (aluminum potassium sulfate)
(1 pound dry weight)

Alum: 3 to 4 ounces
Cream of tartar: 1 ounce
Cold water: 3 to 4 gallons, or enough to cover

Soak clean yarn in lukewarm water for about 15 minutes. Dissolve alum in small quantity of boiling water with cream of tartar. Add to 4 gallons of cold water; put in yarn and slowly bring to simmer in about 30 minutes. Simmer 1 hour longer: let yarn cool in pot. Rinse yarn and dry.

Chrome (potassium dichromate) is the best mordant for bark because it imparts a deep rich color to the dye bath. It is available in granules from drugstores and suppliers. Chrome is more difficult to use than alum and requires care to prevent uneven coloring in the dye bath. This chemical is sensitive to light, so keep the cooking vessel covered during mordanting; the yarn can turn green if light strikes it. Avoid inhaling chrome fumes because they are toxic. Keep ventilation fans going or the mordant in an airy place. Mark all containers of chrome and keep them out of the reach of children or pets.

Measuring the mordant

Dissolving the mordant *Photos by Joyce R. Wilson*

For best results, use chrome as a mordant *before* the yarn is dyed. If you want to achieve a lighter color, reduce the amount of chrome.

CHROME (potassium dichromate)
(1 pound wool dry weight)

Chrome: ½ ounce
Cream of tartar: 1 ounce
Cold water: 3 to 4 gallons, or enough to cover

The process of mordanting with chrome is the same as with alum.

Copper sulfate (or blue vitriol) is available in chunks or in crystals from suppliers; it is inexpensive, and 3 ounces will mordant 3 to 4 pounds of wool. Copper sulfate gives greenish tones to colors; it works well on wool, but is only fair for silk and vegetable fibers.

COPPER SULFATE (blue vitriol)
(1 pound wool dry weight)

Copper sulfate: ⅓ to 1 ounce
Cream of tartar: 1 ounce
Cold water: 3 to 4 gallons

Soak yarn in lukewarm water for about 15 minutes. Dissolve copper sulfate in small quantity of boiling water with cream of tartar and add to cold water. Add yarn and slowly bring to simmer in about 30 minutes. Simmer 1 hour; let yarn cool in pot, then rinse and dry.

Red onion skin is the main dye for this small carryall knapsack; the yarn is chrome mordanted. Some fading of color may be expected, but it will not mar the beauty of the piece. *(Photo by author)*

Tin. Of all the metallic mordants, tin (stannous chloride) is the one that must be used with the greatest care. An excess amount hardens wool and makes it brittle. Tin is costly, but a little goes a long way; three ounces of tin crystals will mordant about five pounds of wool yarn. Tin can be used by itself or in combination with other mordants.

Tin gives bright, clear, and fast colors in the red and yellow hues. It is an excellent mordant for animal fibers, but is poor for linen or cotton. As mentioned, tin can be the mordant itself or may be used on premordanted yarn that is dyed; in this case it acts as a brightening (blooming) agent for color. Tin is poisonous, so keep containers on high shelves out of reach of children or pets.

TIN (stannous chloride)
(1 pound wool dry weight)

Tin: ½ ounce
Cream of tartar: ½ ounce
Cold water: 3 to 4 gallons, or enough to cover

Dissolve tin crystals in small quantity of warm water; dissolve cream of tartar in small quantity of boiling water. Add cream of tartar to cold-water mordant bath first, followed by tin. Add yarn; simmer about 30 minutes. Let yarn cool in pot; rinse yarn with a little soap, then rinse with clear water.

Iron (ferrous sulfate) is also known as green vitriol or copperas. Iron, like tin, can be a mordant itself or it can be added toward the end of the dyeing bath to sadden, or darken, colors. It works well on wool and some vegetable fibers, but is poor for silk. Used alone as a mordant, the iron salts must be evenly distributed over the yarn to avoid streaking, so stir the yarn occasionally. Too much iron will produce a bronzed effect in black hues and will harden wool.

IRON (ferrous sulfate)
(1 pound wool dry weight)

Iron: ½ ounce
Cream of tartar: ½ ounce
Cold water: 3 to 4 gallons, or enough to cover

Use tin mordanting process or, to sadden color, use pre-mordanted dyed yarn and then add iron to last 15 minutes of dyeing. Take wool out of dye bath quickly. Add iron, stir, and put wool back in. Rinse wool thoroughly after cooling.

Mordanting undyed yarn is not difficult, but it depends upon accurate measurements and careful attention to directions. Because no visible coloring of the yarn takes place, the beginner is tempted to rush through the process. Yet, the ultimate color achieved from dye plants depends upon the mordanting and how well it is done. An unevenly mordanted skein of yarn will produce uneven colors when it is dyed.

Different colors may be obtained from plants with different mordants and quantities of mordants. For example, onion skins give one color when used with chrome, another color with alum, and so on. There are limitless possibilities.

HOW TO MORDANT OTHER FIBERS

Even when mordanted, vegetable fibers such as cotton and linen have less affinity for dyes than wool or silk. Often they do not dye as well or as dark.

Mordanting cotton and linen with alum can be done in several ways. An easy method we found satisfactory follows:

COTTON AND LINEN
(1 pound dry weight)

Alum: 4 ounces
Washing soda (sodium carbonate): 1 ounce
Cold water: 4 gallons

Dissolve alum and washing soda in 4 gallons of water. Moisten material, then immerse in solution and stir while heating to boiling point. Boil about 1 to 2 hours, depending upon texture. (Heavy textured yarn needs more boiling than lightweight material.) Let yarn stay in bath overnight. Next day, remove and squeeze out excess moisture.

Another (and perhaps more thorough) mordanting method for vegetable fibers follows:

COTTON AND LINEN
(1 pound dry weight)

Alum: 8 ounces
Washing soda: 2 ounces
Tannic acid: 1 to 2 ounces
Cold water (soft): 4 to 5 gallons*

* For each bath.

Dissolve 4 ounces of alum and 1 ounce of soda in small amount of water. Put in 4 to 5 gallons of water. Wet material and soak overnight in solution. Next day, heat bath gradually; boil 1 hour. Let cloth cool overnight in pot. Next day, squeeze excess moisture from yarn; rinse well. Put cloth in 4 gallons of water and tannic acid. Heat gradually to 160° F. for 1 hour; stir often. Let stand in pot overnight. Use third bath of water with remaining ounce of soda and 4 ounces of alum. Repeat process through step 5.

For mordanting cotton or linen with chrome or tin, use 2 to 4 teaspoonfuls of the mordant to 4 gallons of water. Add the wet, clean material and simmer or boil for 1 to 2 hours. Allow the yarn to cool in the container, then rinse. (Keep the lid on the container if you use chrome.)

With silk, colors will be weaker than with the same amount of dyestuffs used on wool. The quantity of mordants and the process is the same as for wool, except that the water temperature should not exceed 185°F.; simmer 45 minutes.

To mordant silk, follow this recipe:

SILK
(1 pound dry weight)

Alum: 4 ounces
Cream of tartar: 1 ounce
Cold water: 3 to 4 gallons

Wash silk in tepid water. Dissolve alum and cream of tartar in small amount of water and add to cold water bath. Immerse silk and bring water very slowly to 100°F. Remove pot from heat; allow to cool. Let material steep in solution overnight. Dye silk while wet.

MORDANTING WITH AND AFTER THE DYE

We have discussed ways to mordant yarns *before* they are dyed. To mordant and dye *at the same time,* add the mordant to the warm dye bath and stir until dissolved. Add the yarn and simmer or boil for 30 minutes. Next add cream of tartar (2 tablespoons) to the liquid and simmer again for 30 minutes. Rinse yarns in warm water until the rinse becomes clear. Hang the yarn in the shade to dry.

If you prefer to mordant yarns *after* they are dyed, put 3 gallons of warm water in a 5-gallon enamel container, add the mordant, and stir until it is dissolved. Add the dyed yarn and simmer or boil for 30 minutes to 1 hour. Cool the yarn in the pot, rinse, and dry.

If the second mordant is to further ensure colorfastness, the dyed yarns should go back into the original mordant and should simmer an additional 30 minutes. But if you intend to change the color with the second mordant (for example, making yellow yarn green), add half the normal amount of mordant to the fresh material, then add the dyed yarn and simmer for about 40 minutes.

3
Getting
the Dye
Material

Leaves and twigs, barks, flowers, berries, and even weeds are vast storehouses of color. No matter where you live there are plants for dyes. Once you start dyeing with plants, the woods and meadows and your garden and landscape change in meaning. You will never see a flower or leaf without wondering what color it yields in the dye pot. Some work, others don't.

Extracting the color from the plant is done with boiling water, and the process varies, depending upon the material. Generally, plant parts are put in cool water, brought slowly to the boil, and simmered slowly just below the boiling point for a varying period of time. Bark and roots may be cooked immediately or soaked in water overnight before cooking. Leaves and flowers are generally used right after they are picked; however, they may also be soaked overnight before the cooking process. Some dyestuffs need a long period of simmering before they yield a good color; others are ruined by this—the bright red tones of madder, for example. The idea is to get as much of the coloring matter as possible from the plant.

Most plants are used fresh, but some of them—bark or leaves—may be dried. However, I have found the colors more vivid when plants are fresh. Further, storing dried plant parts can be hazardous; if they are not completely dry, they become moldy.

It is always an adventure to see what color a plant will yield in the dye pot; most colors are unique, and to tag them with definite names is impossible. Be ready for surprises. Do not ever think that because a flower is red you will get red from it. Red bougainvillea flower bracts, for example, give beige, and blue morning glories impart a gray-green color to yarn.

As mentioned, plants differ in color content depending on climate and the region where they are grown. The time of year and growing conditions determine the colors that most vegetable materials contain; it seems that hot and somewhat dry weather produces the best plants for dye work. Again, remember that the flower you pick in one geographical region may yield a different color from the same flower picked in another area.

FLOWERS, LEAVES, AND BERRIES

Flowers are perhaps the easiest plant material to collect, and you can grow your own. It is inexpensive, especially from seed (see Chapter 7), and generally most flowers like dahlias and marigolds are easy to grow. For best results, cut flowers at their peak.

Cutting blackberry shoots for dye

Soaking the color from blackberry shoots *Photos by author*

Remember, however, that not all blossoms will yield color in the dye bath.

If you use fresh flowers, you will need about 2½ pounds to 1 pound of wool. Cut the flowers in small pieces and put in an enamel or glass cooking utensil. Cover them with 3 gallons of water; boil for about 15 minutes. Cool. Strain out the cooked flowers; the remaining liquid is the dye.

Dried flowers are also used for dyeing; the drying process is simple, but how you dry them can influence the color they give. To dry blossoms in air, spread them one layer deep on a pan or, better, a wood or wire grid, and put them in a well-ventilated place until they are dry. If the flowers are large, pick the petals so they will dry by themselves. Turn the petals occasionally to hasten drying; sometimes some color is lost in the drying process.

Most flowers can be dried for future use, but some, such as dandelions and dahlias, must be fresh. Keep dried blossoms in porous containers in a dark place and don't try to keep them too long or they will deteriorate.

To extract dye from dried flowers follow the same cooking directions as for fresh flowers.

If you are reluctant to cut garden flowers for dye, grow more than you need, or take weeds such as dandelion, smartweed, dock, or nettle that are seldom missed in the garden. Blackberry plants, too, can become a nuisance, so pick them; young shoots and twigs yield a lovely gray-brown color with alum-mordanted wool or a dark brown color with yarn mordanted with chrome or copper.

Collect leaves when they are mature and have had a season's growth. Leaves for dye are best fresh rather than dried; dryness often causes the loss of color content. For 1 pound of wool, use 2 pounds of leaves; soak them overnight in 3 to 4 gallons of water. The next day boil the leaves in the same water for about 2 hours. Cool. Strain the dye liquid to remove refuse; the liquid is the dye bath. You can omit the overnight soaking of leaves; boil them immediately, if you like, but the color will not be as potent.

Berries for dyeing must be picked when they are completely ripe and used immediately. Use 2 quarts of berries to 1 pound of wool and cover with water; boil gently (about 45 minutes) until the color is removed. Strain, then add enough water to make 4 gallons of dye.

BARKS, ROOTS, AND HULLS

Even before American colonists recognized the dye qualities in trees, American Indians were using them for many purposes. For the colonists the common forest trees were the chief source of brown and gray coloring matter. Home dyers in heavily forested areas collected the tannin-rich bark of alder, hemlock, and maple for brown colors. Other bark, such as birch and oak, were also gathered, depending on what was available in the area. The barks of several trees were probably first employed as mordants because they contained tannin. Later the barks became actual dye substances.

Tree barks yield a complete range of brown to gray tones to wool and light browns to cottons, and while fabrics dyed with bark often do not retain their original color, they do not fade. They become rather darker in tone when exposed to light.

Tree bark may be used fresh or dried. To use it, shred fresh bark and soak it overnight in 2 to 3 gallons of warm water. You will need about 1 pound of bark for each pound of wool. The next day bring the same water to a boil and boil for about 1 hour to extract the color from the bark (add hot water as necessary to maintain a water level), then strain through cheesecloth into another pot. When the dye liquid cools, it is ready for yarn.

Walnut hulls supply the brown dye for this attractive pillow combined with natural animal fibers. *(Design by Ida Grae; photo by Joyce R. Wilson)*

The amount of steeping of the bark in water affects the color. For example, if the process is carried out for several days, the resultant dye liquid will be darker than if the bark was soaked overnight or for a few hours.

Different colors are produced with different premordanted —chrome, copper, tin—yarns. The basic brown hue does not change, but different shades and tints are achieved. (See also Chapter 6.)

To dry bark for future use, let it set in the air after it is chipped into pieces. Do not put it into an oven or fire may occur. Place the bark one layer deep on newspapers, with spaces between the chips so the air will reach all parts. When they are completely dry, put the chips in porous containers (cloth bags or glass jars) and store them in a dry, shady place. Be sure to label the contents on the jars.

The roots of several plants make excellent dyes; try to remove small sections, not all, of the root so the plants may continue to live. Chop the roots (about 1 pound) as finely as possible and soak them overnight in 3 to 4 gallons of water. The next day boil them in the same water for 30 minutes to 1 hour. Strain the dye liquid through cheesecloth; it is now ready for premordanted yarn. If you want to dry roots, follow the same process as for bark drying. You will need about 2 pounds of dried root for 1 pound of wool.

The hulls of black walnuts and pecans have enough tannic acid in them to ensure a colorfast dye without mordanting the yarn. The tannin itself acts as the mordant. Collect nuts when the hulls are mature. Remove the hulls by pounding them with a hammer against a flat rock. (Remember to wear gloves to avoid staining your hands.) Place 1 to 2 pounds of hulls per 1 pound of wool in a 6-gallon enamel container and cover them with 3 to 4 gallons of water to soak overnight. The hulls will soak up water, so the next day add more water to cover. Boil for about 3 hours and then remove the solid matter. The remaining liquid is the dye bath. To dry hulls for future use, follow the same drying process as for bark.

It is the hull of the nut that yields the dye, so collect mature nuts as soon as they fall to the ground, around frost time. Those that remain on the ground through the winter will not make good dye.

LIST OF TREES

Acacia *(Acacia baileyana)* is an evergreen tree native to the tropics and grows to 40 feet. It has feathery, finely cut blue-gray leaves. Its flowers are yellow, and appear in clusters in February. The pods and bark can be used for tan or beige colors for wool.

Alder trees *(Alnus)* were frequently used by European dyers because of their tannin properties. The bark is an excellent source of black coloring matter and produces a wide range of dark colors. *Alnus glutinosa* grows to 50 feet, and has greenish-yellow flower catkins.

Birch trees *(Betula)* are popular ornamental and graceful trees, with white bark on trunks and large branches. There are many kinds of birches, but for dyeing purposes use yellow birch *(Betula lutea)*, canoe birch *(B. papyrifera)*, and sweet birch *(B. lenta)*. The barks yield light brown or black, or muted shades of these colors, depending on when the bark was collected. *By papyrifera* grows to 90 feet, is pyramidal in shape, and has white bark that peels off, and yellow leaves in the fall. *B. lenta* grows to 75 feet, has dense foliage, and is golden yellow in autumn.

Wild Cherry *(Prunus serotina)* grows to 50 to 80 feet and has rough black bark that separates naturally from the tree. Its leaves are 3 to

Soaking oak bark

Dogwood root *Photos by author*

5 inches long and 2 inches wide, and it bears its white flowers in May. The bark contains red coloring matter, and the leaves impart muted shades of gray or green to wool.

Flowering Dogwood *(Cornus florida)* grows to 20 to 30 feet with oval leaves and dense heads of spectacular flowers in spring. The bark of the tree yields a red coloring matter; the root, violet to red. There are several varieties of the species offered.

Eucalyptus is prevalent on the West Coast. These trees may be small or tower to 200 feet. Some species naturally shed their bark; colors (depending on the mordant) vary from umbers to golds.

Hemlocks are narrow-leaved evergreen trees of the genus *Tsuga.* Canadian hemlock *(Tsuga canadensis)* was a favorite dye in the eastern United States because it provided a fine reddish-brown dye. Today there are many varieties of *T. canadensis;* which one you use depends on where you live. *T. canadensis* grows to 90 feet and is evergreen, with dense foliage.

Hickory or mockernut *(Carya tomentosa)* and pecan *(Carya illi-noensis)* are other trees whose bark yields dye. Hickory is especially noted for its yellow color, and pecan hulls are used for brown coloring. *C. illinoensis* grows to 70 feet and is sprawling and grace-ful, with long, narrow leaflets. *C. tomentosa* is a 90-foot, round-headed tree with dense compound leaves and 5 to 9 leaflets.

Oaks *(Quercus),* with 50 kinds available in this country, are another dye source. Quercitron from *Quercus velutina* is famous for the fast and bright yellow colors it gives to textiles. White oak *(Q. alba)* and red oak *(Q. rubra)* are also used. *Q. velutina,* sometimes also called black oak, grows to 150 feet and is rounded and dense; the foliage is dark green, turning red in the fall.

Dogwood root chopped and soaking overnight

Straining the dye from dogwood root *Photos by Joyce R. Wilson*

Peach *(Prunus persica)* grows to 25 feet, with light green, pointed leaves. Peach leaves yield shades of yellow with alum-mordanted wool.

Sassafras *(Sassafras albidum)* bark is a valuable source of orange-brown dye. This deciduous tree grows to about 50 feet, with a heavy trunk and rather short branches. Its leaves are 3 to 7 inches long and 2 to 4 inches wide, oval or lobed on one side or lobed on both sides. The foliage turns scarlet in the fall.

Sumac *(Rhus glabra)* was an important tree valued in early America for its leaves as mordants. Later the bark was used as a local dye for drab browns and slate colors. *R. glabra* is a 20-foot deciduous tree with 2- to 5-inch toothed leaflets that are deep green above and white below; it turns red in the fall.

American colonists knew about the rich browns available from walnut as early as 1668. Although there are basic color differences between white walnut, or butternut *(Juglans cinerea),* and black walnut *(J. nigra),* the resultant dyes from both will be a shade of brown. *J. nigra* is a large tree that grows to 150 feet, with furrowed, blackish-brown bark and 2- to 5-inch leaves in leaflets. *J. cinerea* grows to 50 feet; it is a broad, spreading tree with smaller leaflets than *J. nigra.*

Our experiments with apple bark *(Malus)* gave us a yellow color with alum-mordanted wool and a yellowish-tan with chrome wool. When we prepared dogwood root *(Cornus florida),* we expected a violet color. However, the color was more brown than the elusive violet we were seeking. With lombardy poplar leaves *(Populus nigra* 'Italica') we were pleasantly surprised with a lovely muted green color on alum-mordanted wool.

GRASSES AND WEEDS

Many grasses and weeds are free for the taking and make excellent dyes. These include broom sedge (Andropogon virginicus) and cane (Arundinaria macrosperma), which grows along river banks and gives wool shades of green or yellow.

Generally, use the chopped stalks and leaves of the plants. Cut them into small pieces, soak them for a few hours, and boil. To use grasses and weeds dry, follow the drying method for barks and then pulverize the material in a mortar and pestle after it is dried. Collect grasses between late spring and the first frost.

Bracken (Pteridium aquilinum)
Broom sedge (Andropogon virginicus)
Cane (Arundinaria macrosperma)
Dandelion (Taraxacum officinale)*
Dock (Rumex obtusifolius)*
Nettle (Urtica dioica)
Queen Anne's lace (Daucus carota)
Saint-John's-wort (Hypericum perforatum)
Smartweed (Polygonum hydropiper)

STEMS, TWIGS, AND VINES

Many dyes can be obtained from plant stems, twigs, and vines; use them fresh or dry them by tying them in bunches and hanging them from ceiling rafters in a well-ventilated place. Do not dry these materials in an oven because of the danger of fire. To use

* Use roots.

fresh, cut up the plant parts (about 2 pounds per pound of wool) and soak in 3 to 4 gallons of water overnight; next day boil in the same water for 1 hour. Strain out the refuse; the remaining liquid is the dye bath.

These materials can be easily collected, and taking them does not harm the tree or shrub or plant. Gather them at peak season from mature plants rather than from seedlings.

We have found it best to use stems and twigs fresh, for when dried they seem to lose much color.

HOUSEHOLD ITEMS

Ground coffee beans and tea leaves, beets, and spinach all contain dye. So do onion skins, but the color will vary with the type of onion. Red skins yield a brown color; yellow skins give shades of yellow. (See Chapter 8 for recipes.)

LICHENS

If you have hiked through the woods you have undoubtedly seen lichens on trees and soil. Lichens are plants that manufacture their own chlorophyll, unlike most plants, and they resemble fungus and are often classified as mosses, but they are different. Most lichens have distinctive and pale yellowish-green or gray colors without differentiation between leaves and stems. Unlike mosses, which have primitive leaves and stems and grow in damp places, lichens inhabit sunny places. Generally the plants are round, small, and scattered, although clusters do appear on woods. They may be shrubby, crustlike, or leaflike.

Ideal collecting places for lichens are open dry woods and

Yellow onion skin is the predominate dye in this tam; the brown-black color is from blackberry shoots. *(Design by Charlene Jackson; photo by Joyce R. Wilson)*

A macramé hanging, using indigo and sage, laced on wood sticks with plant pods; a total, beautiful organic hanging. *(Design by Charlene Jackson; photo by Joyce R. Wilson)*

rocks through the southern United States, the Pacific Coast, the Ohio River valley, and Canada.

To collect lichens for dyeing, use a knife or hammer and a chisel. Lichens are fairly firm and leathery when dry, but they can be very brittle. When moistened, they are easier to collect. Put lichens in cloth or paper sacks if dry (you can store them for some time). If wet, dry them first by spreading them out on newspapers. Do not put lichens in plastic containers as the moisture within the bag will discolor them.

Whenever you collect lichens for dye, do not completely destroy small or rare colonies. Leave some to continue the species; these are slow-growing plants. Obtain permission to collect if you are in a state or national park.

The American Indians used lichens for dyes, and almost all kinds are satisfactory. Yarn for lichen dyeing does not need to be mordanted. However, most lichens need a soaking time before they are boiled to release their various red, brown, or orange shades.

Here are some lichens you might want to try:

Parmelia saxatilis has lobes tipped with angular white markings and is weakly ridged. The thallus is white to green-gray. This lichen is found on both the Pacific and East coasts. *P. saxatilis* yields a slightly reddish-brown color.

P. omphalodes (brown lichen) has an upper cortex ridged and marked with white. The thallus is greenish or white, gray to brown. This lichen is found in alpine locations and gives a clean, dark brown color.

P. centrifuga (green lichen) has a lower white surface, and the thallus is pale greenish-yellow. This lichen is found along the northern Great Lakes shoreline and in the Appalachians and yields a slightly reddish-brown color.

Alectoria sarmentosa is greenish yellow, pendulous, and stiff. It is common on trees in mountains and gives a fine greenish-yellow color.

Cetraria glauca grows in big thin slices and yields a yellow to yellow-brown color.

These are only a sampling of the many lichens that can be used for dyeing.

4
The
Dyeing
Process

Once you have gathered plant materials and extracted color from them, the actual dyeing process is simple. Simmer mordanted yarn in the prepared dyestuff liquid. However, make sure the solution is lukewarm (100°F.) and of sufficient amount to cover the yarns when you put them into it. Additional water added to the dye bath later will produce lighter shades of color. Aluminum, tin, or iron pots will affect the dye color, so as previously mentioned use enamel or glass cooking vessels, or the 10-quart canners from hardware stores.

Water temperatures are very important when preparing dye baths because although some fibers can tolerate boiling, others will be ruined by it. Lukewarm water temperatures range from 95°F. to 105°F. Temperatures over 145°F. are considered hot, and simmering temperatures vary from 180°F. to 210°F. (Water boils at 212°F.)

Before you start the dye process be sure the skeins of washed yarns are adequately tied; otherwise they may come loose in the dye bath, and it will take hours to get them together. Do not tie the skeins tightly; the fixative agent will not be able to penetrate all parts of the yarn and an uneven dye will result.

The following dye process is the one that we have used most successfully with a number of plant materials:

1 Wet yarn.
2 Pour dye into enamel or glass pot. (There should be 4 to 4½ gallons of dye bath per pound of wool.)
3 Put in wet yarn.
4 Keep lid on pot (optional).
5 Bring to simmer within 20 to 30 minutes.
6 Simmer for 1 hour, stirring back and forth every 3 to 5 minutes
7 Cool in pot.
8 Rinse yarn with water until water runs clear (rinse water should be of same temperature as dye bath).
9 Wash yarn with soap.
10 Rinse yarn with water again.
11 Dry yarn in shade.

Increase or decrease dyestuffs to change color, but *never change the timing.* Generally, two or three rinses will be needed, and the last rinse should be in lukewarm water.

Dry all yarns out of direct heat and light; they can be dried outside in the shade or inside. *Never* put them in a clothes dryer.

Dye solutions (that you want to use later) will spoil at room temperature within a few days unless precautions are taken to preserve them. To keep them for several days, put them in glass jars and store in a cool, shady place or put in a refrigerator. (Never store dyes in metal containers.)

Be wary of any vegetable dyes you think are spoiled; they will change the color of the yarn and give off toxic fumes.

BLOOMING AND SADDENING WOOL

Blooming or brightening a color should be done during the last ten to twenty minutes of dyeing previously mordanted wool. Do it in the following way:

Dissolve ½ ounce of tin crystals in water. Dissolve ½ ounce of cream of tartar in water. Turn off heat and remove yarn from dye bath. Add dissolved tin and cream of tartar to dye bath and stir. Quickly put wool back in dye bath and simmer 10 to 20 minutes. Remove yarn and rinse it with a little soap until water is clear.

Saddening wool is another during-the-dye process and imparts lovely muted shades to yarn. It is done as follows:

Dissolve ½ ounce of iron salts in water. Dissolve ½ ounce of cream of tartar in water. Turn off heat and remove yarn from dye bath. Add iron and cream of tartar to dye bath. Quickly put wool back in dye and simmer 10 to 15 minutes. Remove yarn and rinse it with soap until water is clear.

NOTES ON DYED COLORS

Yellows fade the fastest, are fast with chrome and tin, and turn gold and greenish gold with chrome. The clearest yellows come from safflower thistles and peach leaves.

Yellow-oranges are fastest with chrome and tin (especially to light), turn brownish and greenish brown with chrome, and are brightened with tin.

Oranges and reds are very fast from madder and cochineal (see Chapter 5). True red can be obtained from madder and alum plus a little cochineal. (Madder is lighter, clearer, and less brown if simmered below 160°F.) Chrome turns madder colors brown, while tin turns madder colors more orange and rust.

Reds and purples are clearer with cochineal and cream of tartar. Tin brightens further. Chrome turns cochineal to deeper purples.

Greens. Light indigo over clear yellow gives bright green. The darker the indigo dye, the deeper the green. To get olive green without indigo, mordant a yellow with chrome plus ¼ ounce of iron per pound of wool (you may add a little more) in the last 10 minutes of dyeing. A yellow will become gray-green if it is mordanted with alum plus ½ ounce of iron or copper sulfate. Tin brightens.

Browns are light, fast with most mordants, darkened and grayed with chrome, and brightened toward oranges and yellows with tin.

Grays and blacks. For black, overdye walnut brown with dark indigo. For a truer black, overdye yellow with red and then blue. Rhododendron leaves give the best light gray. Add ¼ ounce of iron per pound of wool in the last 10 minutes of dyeing.

COLORFASTNESS

Although I have heard many craftsmen say they do not care if color fades somewhat, most people consider fastness or permanence of a dye very important. However, not all vegetable dyes are absolutely colorfast under all situations. Colorfastness depends on the amount of washing, how much sunlight the dye is exposed to, and so on. One method of dyeing may produce a colorfast material, another method may not, and not all fibers will hold color. We work so much with wool because its resulting colors seem to change the least; but, in fact, with time they mellow. Cotton, on the other hand, is more likely to fade.

What the product is used for is another consideration. For wearing apparel, it would be well within reason to have color that fades somewhat as it would be for a hooked rug. But for weavings and wall hangings, a color change may be undesirable.

The simplest way to test dyed yarn for colorfastness is to expose a piece of it to direct light for a period of time. Then put the piece next to a piece that had no light. For waterfastness, wash a swatch under ordinary washing conditions and compare it with a piece of unwashed yarn.

TOP-DYEING

Part of the fun of dyeing yarns with natural materials is to create your own colors—that is, to dip material into two different colored dye baths to obtain the desired hue. Basically, you are re-dyeing already dyed yarns to deepen or alter the color.

The secret of this process is to use thoroughly mordanted yarns and start with good clear colors. If you want a good green, start with a bright yellow and top it with bright blue. Some plant materials, such as fustic and goldenrod, give excellent yellows. A better green can be created by first dyeing with indigo and then top-dyeing with yellow.

Indigo and madder are the workhorses of the top-dyeing process because with them you can get all sorts of lovely reds and oranges (madder) and greens and blues (indigo). Combinations of colors are apt to be tricky at first, so few set rules can be given. Experiment and observe; color mixing is an art in itself.

5
Commercial Woods, Prepared Plant Materials

In the eighteenth century the general store carried madder, logwood, fustic, and cutch for home dyers, since commercial dyeing had not yet started. Today the basic products remain the same, sold as bark chips or as powdered extracts; they are available at yarn shops or from botanical supply companies.

Because these woods were so extensively used for dyeing, innumerable recipes for madder, logwood, fustic, cutch, and indigo are still available. Old dye books give many formulas for logwood and for combining madder with other dyes and different mordants to achieve various red to orange hues. Some of the old recipes are quite complicated, yet all are still valid (with modifications). Thus, what we are doing today with these plant materials is not much different from the old practices, and although processes may change slightly, these plants still possess valuable dyes.

MADDER

Madder (*Rubia tinctorum*) is native to Asia Minor and yields an excellent red dye. The roots of the plant contain alizarin, orange-red crystals. Alizarin is almost insoluble in water but is readily soluble in alkaline solutions. When joined with alum, alizarin produces a lovely rose color. Cultivation of the plant began in America about 1800, but nothing came of it, either because of climatic conditions or perhaps lack of perseverance.

Madder is a suitable dye for almost all natural fibers, and the colorfastness is excellent. As mentioned, the mordant used on the yarn will determine the resultant color. With tin, for example, madder root yields a bright red or pink-red color, and with chrome you get lovely orange and rust hues. (Store madder in glass jars in a dry place.)

RECIPE FOR RED
(*1 pound wool dry weight*)

Madder: 8 ounces
Cold water: 4 gallons

Crush and soak madder roots overnight in water to cover. Next morning, boil roots for about 30 minutes. Pour the hot liquid into a pot; add cool water to make 4 gallons. Cool. Squeeze out and rinse alum-mordanted yarn, then immerse in dye bath. Boil for about 45 minutes. Rinse yarn and dry.

RECIPE FOR ORANGE
(1 pound wool dry weight)

Madder: 4 ounces
Cold water: 4 gallons

Grind madder root and cook with 2 cups of water for 10 minutes at 160°F. Strain dye liquid into enamel or glass pot and add cold water to make 4 gallons solution. Cool. Add chrome-mordanted yarn and bring solution to 200°F.; simmer 1 hour. Let yarn cool in dye bath. Remove yarn and rinse.

Madder *Photo by author*

craftsman who made this shawl was an expert colorist; the combina-
of dahlia, madder, and red onion skin dyes creates a beautiful composi-
(Photo by author)

LOGWOOD

Logwood (*Haematoxylon campechianum*) is a native tree of Mexico, Honduras, the West Indies, and South America. The name of the plant genus comes from the Greek and refers to the blood-red color of the heartwood. The wood contains two brown substances: quercetin and tannin. The salts are colorless until they are exposed to oxygen and an alkaline base; then they produce reds, blues, and purple dyes, depending on the mordant used.

Logwood yields a good brown dye to unmordanted yarn that is fairly colorfast, but for blue, colorfastness is only fair. The wood is available in chips or as extracts (finely ground chips).

RECIPE FOR VIOLET
(1 pound wool dry weight)

Logwood chips: 1½ ounces
Cold water: 4 gallons

Soak chips overnight in water to cover; boil next day for 30 minutes. Strain dye liquid into enamel or glass pot and add cool water to make 4-gallon solution. Cool. Add tin-mordanted yarn and bring solution to 200°F.; simmer 1 hour. Let yarn cool in pot. Remove yarn and rinse.

FUSTIC

Fustic (*Morus tinctoria* or *Chlorophora tinctoria*) makes an excellent yellow dye. It is a member of the mulberry family, native to Brazil and Jamaica. (A close second to fustic is the American smoke tree, *Cotinus coggygria,* which is also a good source of yellow dye.) Fustic bark chips used with an alum-mordanted material give a bright yellow color to all natural fibers except linen. Colorfastness is excellent. Orange or rust hues are the result when you use fustic with indigo and alum-mordanted yarns.

RECIPE FOR BRIGHT YELLOW
(1 pound wool dry weight)

Fustic: ½ ounce
Cold water: 4 gallons

Dissolve fustic extract in small amount of water; add to 4 gallons of cool water. Squeeze out and rinse chrome-mordanted wool and immerse in dye bath. Boil for about 45 minutes. Rinse yarn and dry.

Fustic chips *Photo by author*

INDIGO

Indigo (*Indigofera tinctoria*) is a leguminous plant from India, and wild indigo (*Baptisia tinctoria*) grows from Canada to Carolina. The renowned blue dye is obtained from the leaves of the plant. It is available from suppliers in cake form or powdered; if possible select the latter kind. Otherwise you will have to grind the cake into powder, and it is a messy job.

Indigo does not require mordanted yarn and it is not soluble in water; indigo must first be changed by a reducing agent and then dissolved in alkali so that wool or cotton fiber can absorb it. The dyeing process with indigo is somewhat different than with other dye plants. A solution is prepared first, then combined with a dye bath. To dye, the material is dipped in the dye bath and then held in the air (you can see the blue coloring start at the bottom and run to the top as air strikes it). To get shades of blue, the yarn is dipped in the dye bath (but no more than three times).

There are several methods for indigo dyeing, but the hydro-sulfite process is the most satisfactory:

STOCK SOLUTION FOR INDIGO
(Will dye about 2 pounds wool dry weight)

Cold water: 1 cup
Powdered indigo: 1 ounce
Sodium hydrosulfite: 1 ounce
Lye solution: 3¼ ounces (½ ounce lye to ¼ cup water)
Glue solution: 3½ ounces glue to 1 quart water

Mix indigo with water (use heavy glass or enamel vessel). Stir in sodium hydrosulfite gradually and let mixture stand for 10 minutes. Mix in lye solution. Set pot inside another pot with water and heat slowly to 120°F. within 5 minutes (stir slowly while heating). Put solution in jar, cover tightly (solution should be golden brown), and wait at least 1 hour before using.

To prepare the dye bath:

Stir stock in jar gently and measure out amount needed (½ amount in jar for 1 pound of wool). Add stock to 3 to 4 gallons of hot (120°F) water and stir gently. Add 1 ounce sodium hydrosulfite, 1 ounce ammonia, and 3 ounces glue solution. Remove scum from top of dye bath, if any. Dye bath should appear clear green.

To dye yarn:

Soak yarn in lukewarm water. Put yarn in dye bath for 15 minutes, maintaining 120°F., then take out of pot and air for 15 minutes (hang on pole and turn constantly). Dip twice to make colorfast and not more than three times to get darker. Rinse yarn in lukewarm water with 2 tablespoons of vinegar to stop oxidation.

If the dye bath turns blue as you use it, add one-half amount of chemicals again (sodium hydrosulfite, ammonia, glue).

CUTCH

Cutch (catechu) is an Asiatic tree, and is one of the oldest sources of brown dye; it was used in Indian calico printing long before it was recognized in Europe or America. Two Asiatic trees are known as cutch: *Acacia catechu* and *Areca catechu* (the heartwood and pods are used). Cutch is available as a powder and is easily soluble in boiling water; unlike bark it does not have to be soaked overnight.

Cutch is used mainly as a brown dye, for which it depends entirely on its tannic acid properties. Cutch can be used without a mordant for a fine rust color with excellent colorfastness.

Gambier (*Uncaria gambir*), a vine from India, is also sometimes called cutch; the leaves and twigs contain the brown dye.

RECIPE FOR RICH BROWN
(1 pound wool dry weight)

Cutch extract: 4 ounces
Copper sulfate: ½ ounce
Chrome: ½ ounce
Cold water: 8 gallons

Boil cutch and copper sulfate in 4 gallons of cold water. When dissolved and still hot, immerse yarn in solution. Let stand overnight. In the morning, take yarn from solution, squeeze, and put in hot bath of chrome and 4 gallons of water. Simmer for 45 minutes. Rinse yarn and dry.

COCHINEAL

Cochineal is the dried bodies—crushed and pulverized—of the insect *Dactylopius coccus*. The Spaniards, who discovered the material in Mexico in the early 1500s (the natives were using cochineal as a face dye), thought it was the seeds of a plant. In the 1700s it was, along with the cheaper madder, a staple red dye. Cochineal's coloring constituent is carminic acid, which produces fine pinks, crimsons, and reds on wool or silk that has been mordanted with alum or tin.

These are the cochineal recipes we have tried:

RECIPE FOR AMERICAN BEAUTY RED
(1 pound wool dry weight)

Cochineal: 1 ounce
Cold water: 4 gallons

Boil cochineal in water to cover for 15 minutes; strain. Add extract to 4 gallons of cold water; put alum-mordanted yarn in solution and boil for about 2 hours.

RECIPE FOR MAGENTA
(1 pound wool dry weight)

Cochineal: 2 ounces
Vinegar: 1 teaspoon
Cold water: 4 gallons

Boil cochineal and vinegar in small amount of water for 10 minutes; strain. Add extract to 4 gallons of cold water. Put chrome-mordanted yarn in solution and boil for 1½ hours.

RECIPE FOR BRIGHT ORANGE
(1 pound wool dry weight)

Fustic: ½ ounce
Cold water: 4 gallons
Cochineal: 2 ounces
Salt: 1 teaspoon

Dissolve fustic in small amount of water and add to 4 gallons of cold water. Add tin-mordanted yarn and boil for 30 minutes. Dissolve cochineal and salt in small amount of water and add to dye bath. Boil 30 minutes.

For other recipes see Chapter 8.

6
Color

Dyeing yarns with vegetable materials is a variable process, and this creation of your own color is the fun and excitement of it all.

To make your own colors, it is necessary to know something about color and how it works. Newton's experiment with a prism and a beam of light revealed that light is composed of waves of different lengths traveling at different speeds. These waves are the colors of the visible spectrum. If you do this experiment yourself you will see that the colors are always arranged with red (the longest wavelength) at one end and violet (the shortest) at the other end. In between are orange, yellow, green, blue, and indigo. Further experiments revealed that red, green, and violet are the primary

This baby's cap is a combination of indigo and bougainvillea dye. The pattern is hardly intricate, yet the piece is attractive. Rhododendron leaves supply the dark color. *(Design by Charlene Jackson; photo by Joyce R. Wilson)*

colors of the visible spectrum. In 1730, applying Newton's principle to pigment rather than to light, the German painter Jacob Le Bon discovered the primary nature of red, blue, and yellow.

Brewster, a Scottish physician, determined that there are two separate systems in the nature of color: the additive light system, with all colors from white, and the subtractive pigment system— the one that concerns us—in which only reflected rays produce a visual color.

SOME COLOR BASICS

Anyone working with dyes is concerned with color in textiles; he is not concerned with the physiological aspect of the way the human eye perceives color, or with the psychology of color, but with what happens when two or more dyes or pigments are mixed. And the color principle that governs the mixing of pigments and dyes is based on the Le Bon color triangle of red, blue, and yellow, the primary colors in mixing. For example, red and blue give purple, blue and yellow yield green, and yellow and red produce orange. These then are the six colors in the spectrum. But really identifying and recognizing these colors involves other principles, too, because red is not just red; it can be purple-red or yellow-red, depending on hue, value, intensity, tint, and shade.

Hue (for example, red, blue, or orange) is the name of the color. Hues can be classified as *warm*—yellows, oranges, scarlets, crimsons, and their derivatives—or *cool*—blues, greens, purples, and their derivatives.

Value, or *tone*, is the lightness or darkness of the color; *intensity*, or *saturation*, indicates the purity or brightness of a hue.

One end of the intensity scale will be light and bright, the other end will be dulled or neutral.

Tint refers to the paleness of a color; a color is mixed with white. *Shade* is the darkness of a color. To get a shade, mix a color with black. Thus, red and white gives you a tint of red called pink, red and black yields a shade of red called maroon. (Mixtures of a hue with white and black give grayed colors because black is a mixture of the three primary colors.)

Because an infinite range of colors is possible, depending on the character of the dyes or pigments, you must experiment. Mix the three primary pigments together to get black. (Prove this by dipping wool into a blue dye first, then a red, and ending with a yellow dye bath.) You can get a gray by mixing black and white. To lighten add white, and to darken add more black. Gray is also produced by combining hues directly opposite each other on the color wheel.

SOME COLOR COMBINATIONS

Blue and red: Purple
Blue and brown: Dull brown
Blue and green: Turquoise
Yellow and red: Orange
Yellow and blue: Green
Yellow and brown: Gold-brown
Yellow and purple: Yellowish green
Green and brown: Olive green
Orange and brown: Dark brown
Orange and green: Yellowish green

Trying to duplicate the colors of fabrics dyed with natural materials is almost impossible because, as we have discussed, a plant's color content depends on many things. Generally, mature plants have the greatest quantity of dye. Most dye plants produce yellows, browns, grays, oranges, and reds of innumerable intensities and values.

The dyer-handweaver's finished product will be a total composition that includes several different-colored yarns. How he weaves the colors into the composition is important, for the eye sees one color one way against a specific background of, say, red against green, and another way when red is placed against blue. The eye seeks balance, and so balance of contrasts is necessary for good color harmony.

USING COLOR IN COMPOSITIONS

Generally, a textile composition should have one predominating color, either a single color or a mixture of associated colors that *visually* look like one color. Small areas of different colors closely placed together give the total effect of a color that would result if the same colors were mixed as a dye. And the closer a fabric is to the eye, the smaller the color spots must be to achieve the desired harmony. Thus, mixing comes off best when very fine yarns are used.

If fine fibers are put into variously colored dyes, then mixed and carded together, the fiber will be totally blended, and yarn spun with these fibers will take on a solid-colored appearance when viewed from afar. A textile will also appear solid colored if a blend of two tones, alternated in the warp and weft, is used. Depth is added to what is really not a solid color but appears as such. Thus the eye can be fooled if you know the colors and can place controlled amounts of contrasting hues next to each other. (Checks, plaids, and stripes are examples of such a treatment.)

When you are creating your composition, remember that primary and secondary colors produce afterimages in the eye; these afterimages are reflected on white or gray as the eye moves from one hue to the other. If the contrast or afterimage color is not supplied for relief, the results are often not desirable. You can intensify colors in a composition by placing *contrasting* colors side by side. When two closely related colors are placed next to each other, there is a marked reduction in their brilliance, and they are slightly grayed. Unrelated colors that are placed side by side in a composition produce some distortion.

Warm and cool colors also affect the textile composition. The warm colors—yellow, orange, and red—appear to move forward to the viewer; dark values or cool colors—violet, blue, and green—are pushed to the background. (Look at flowers in the garden: red and orange flowers always appear up front, and the blue flowers naturally move to the background.) This advancing and receding of color vitally affects how the rough surface of a textile will appear as a whole composition.

The colors in a composition will also be affected by the kind of light shining on it. Colored textiles appear quite different under sunlight, artificial light, and so on. For example, red will appear clear in daylight, yellow-red under incandescent light, and bluish-red with fluorescent light. Daylight or white light contains all wavelengths, so all but the red will be absorbed; red will be the color you will see. Incandescent light is yellow, so light waves of yellow-red will be seen, and blue fluorescent light always reflects blue-red light.

The texture of the yarn can also influence how light is distributed on the surface of a fabric. Fold a fabric and notice how the textural qualities are emphasized. Light playing on a smooth red fabric makes it appear much lighter in color than a rough tweed having the same red hue.

7
Dyer's
Garden

Although dye plants like grasses, weeds, and wild flowers can be gathered at roadsides and in forests, you will have to grow the common garden flowers—dahlias, chrysanthemums, etc. Even the dearest friend will not let you strip the garden—unless, of course, you promise a weaving.

Your own dyer's garden, where numerous plants can be grown to perfection, is a natural storehouse of color. And even if you think you can't grow a thing, you'll be surprised how many flowers can be grown with almost no care. If you fail in the garden (but you shouldn't if you read this chapter), you will no doubt have volunteers: weeds that are suitable for dyeing.

The rudimentary aspects of gardening follow: They are not meant to be complete (there are numerous garden books if you want to delve further), but following these suggestions will get you started in the right direction.

PERENNIALS AND ANNUALS

Annuals, such as petunias and nasturtiums, are plants that last for a season. Perennials survive from year to year, sprouting new growth each spring. In between perennials and annuals is a small group of plants called biennials (for example, hollyhocks, a good dye plant), which last for two years.

Perennials are your best bet; one year you can use them for dyeing and the next year for outdoor display. Although you can start plants from seed, and a section follows that tells you how, it is easier (but not cheaper) to buy small plants at the local nursery when they are ready for planting. With reasonable care and depending on the kind of perennial, you will have some flowers the same year and an abundant supply the following year. However, if you want to be sure of blooms the first year, annuals are almost fool-proof.

Blooming-size perennials and annuals are available in cans, flats, pots, or freshly dug at your local nursery. Small plants generally transplant easily and grow vigorously; the basic prerequisite for getting them to bloom is a good soil bed in a sunny location. The bottom soil is usually heavy, so break it up and add some sand, cinders, lime, or quantities of ashes. At the same time, work compost humus (decayed leaves and so forth) into the soil. If the soil is sandy add some leaf mold and humus.

It is best to start perennials in spring, but this time can vary with the variety. In cold climates early spring is the best time. The fall months are satisfactory too, but put plants in early enough so that the roots have time to get established before the ground freezes. Mild-climate planting can be done in late autumn, when plants are dormant, or in early spring.

If plants are in a flat (a 16″ x 20″ shallow wood box), remove each one wih a piece of root. Never crowd plants in the garden; four to six inches apart is fine for most.

When setting plants in place, firm but do not compact the soil around the collar of the plant, so water can get to the roots. Water thoroughly the first few weeks until the plants become established. After that routine watering can be started. Perennials and annuals need lots of water; a quick sprinkling will not produce bountiful flowers. Water thoroughly and heavily to really soak the soil. It takes four hours for water to penetrate sixteen inches of soil.

In cold climates, mulch the plants the first winter after the ground has frozen. Mulching shades the soil and keeps it from the freezing and thawing that can cause plants to heave from the ground. (There are many mulching materials: fir bark, sawdust, and compost.) In spring, remove the mulch and feed with a liquid plant food. I use a mild solution of 5–5–10.

LIST OF PERENNIAL AND ANNUAL FLOWERS

Alkanet (*Alkanna tinctoria*). These spreading perennials are about 6 inches high, with roughly hairy oblong leaves and blue flowers in June. The very large root yields a red dye.

Marigold American or **African** (*Tagetes erecta*). These annuals are robust, trouble-free plants that grow from 6 to 40 inches in height. The flowers range in color from yellow to gold to orange and bloom from early summer to frost if you keep picking off old flowers. Plant seedlings deep in a rich soil and keep well watered. Marigolds are easy to grow from seed; always give them plenty of sunshine for maximum bloom.

Bloodroot (*Sanguinaria canadensis*). This perennial is a member of the poppy family. It gets its common name from the red juice that flows from cut roots and stems. These plants have big, deeply lobed leaves and small white- or pink-tinged flowers in early spring. Bloodroot likes a damp shady place. The roots contain red resin.

Butterfly weed (*Asclepias tuberosa*). This perennial has 30-inch stems and oblong, lancelike leaves. The flowers are carried in terminal umbels and are orange or yellow in September. When powdered, the dried root yields a yellowish-brown color.

Calliopsis (*Coreopsis tinctoria*). A 36-inch annual with yellow, orange, or reddish flowers banded with contrasting colors, calliopsis is a member of the sunflower family. Remove old flowers to prolong bloom through the summer. Seed can be sown in place in almost any soil that is kept moderately moist. This plant needs sun.

Chamomile (*Anthemis nobilis*). This perennial is a ground cover that forms a spreading mat of aromatic leaves. The summer-blooming flower heads resemble small buttons. Chamomile will take shade or some sun, and needs an evenly moist soil. *A. tinctoria* is known as golden marguerite and is a good dye plant. It grows to 36 inches in height with light green leaves and golden-yellow, daisylike flowers in summer. The plant needs full sun and is easily grown from seed. The active constituent of the plant is a volatile pale blue oil that becomes yellow with time; excessive drying dissipates the color matter.

Butterfly weed *Photo by Ro*

A handsome pillow made completely from natural dyes: tickseed (coreopsis), tea, and indigo. Tickseed supplied the yellow, and saddened with iron, the green color. *(Design by Batina Grae; photo by author)*

China aster (*Callistephus chinensis*). This is an annual that grows to about 30 inches and has many different flower forms in colors from white to pink to red to lavender in summer. The plants grow in almost any soil in full sun; do not overwater, or aster wilt may result.

Chrysanthemum. This large group of plants includes pyrethrum (*Chrysanthemum coccineum*), marguerite (*C. frutescens*), Shasta daisy (*C. maximum*), and florist's chrysanthemum (*C. morifolium*). Pyrethrums are perennials that grow to about 36 inches and have daisylike flowers of red, white, or pink. Bloom starts in late April, and if the plant is cut back, usually a second crops starts in late summer. These plants need summer heat, sun, and lots of water. Sow seeds in spring. Marguerites are fast-growing perennials that are tender in cold climates. The flowers are generally white or yellow and bloom in summer. Give the plants a light soil and full sun. Shasta daisies are tough perennials that grow 24 to 48 inches high. The flowers have white or gold centers. Set the plants out in early spring in a well-drained rich soil and keep them well watered. Shasta daisies will tolerate some shade and still bloom.

Coneflower (*Rudbeckia;* also called black-eyed Susan). Garden rudbeckias are descendants of wild plants from the eastern United States. The plants grow to 40 inches, with daisylike flowers, and need moist rich soil and plenty of sun.

Cornflower (bachelor's button) (*Centaurea cyanus*). This plant grows 1 to 3 inches and has hairy stems, long narrow leaves, and brilliant blue flowers. The cornflower grows wild in any soil. Its petals contain blue coloring matter.

Dahlia. An enormous group of perennials grown from tubers, most are all hybrids now available in many flower forms and colors, but for dyeing the orange- and yellow-colored flowers are the most commonly used. Tubers must be planted at least 12 inches deep after frost is over and the soil is warm. Put the tubers in full sun and prepare a good potting soil of peat moss, loam, and lots of humus. Seeds can be started indoors earlier in hotbeds. Give the plants plenty of water but little feeding. Store the tubers in the fall, after the tops have turned yellow: cut to about 4 inches above the ground, and lift carefully. Shake off soil, let the tubers dry in sun, and then divide them immediately or store them in a cool (40° F. to 50° F.) dry place, covered with sand and sawdust. A few weeks before planting in the spring, separate the tubers, leaving a piece of stalk with each tuber. Be sure to cut so each tuber has a growing eye.

Day lily *(Hemerocallis)*. This perennial has fleshy roots, swordlike leaves, and lilylike flowers that are usually orange or yellow. The day lily grows in almost any soil, takes sun or part sun, and likes plenty of water while blooming (but not so much at other times). Divide the plants in early spring or late fall.

Goldenrod *(Solidago canadensis)*. A perennial with 36-inch stems and plume-yellow flowers. Goldenrod is easily grown in most soils; it prefers a somewhat dryish condition. The root contains yellow juice.

Hollyhock *(Althaea rosea)*. This is a biennial or a short-lived perennial that has been cultivated since 1573. The plants grow to 10 feet in height, with spikes of large, rose-colored flowers. The leaves are round, somewhat heart shaped. Grow hollyhocks against a fence or wall or in back of borders. The plants grow in almost any soil, thrive in sun, and bloom in summer. You can get deep purple-black coloring matter from the flower petals.

Larkspur (*Delphinium ajacis*). This is an annual with stems about 18 inches long and pink-purple or blue flowers. Larkspur needs a sandy soil and moderate watering. The seeds are poisonous. The juice of the petals mixed with alum mordant gives a nice blue dye.

Lily of the valley (*Convallaria majalis*). A perennial that grows from a tiny corm, the plant has small, fragrant, white waxy flowers and broad, dark green basal leaves. Plant the corms in rich soil in November or December, about 2 inches deep. The plants need winter chilling to grow. Lily of the valley is spring blooming and thrives in a partially bright place with plenty of water.

Lupine (*Lupinus*). An annual or perennial, this plant has leaves divided into leaflets and sweet pea-type flowers that are borne in dense spikes at the end of stems. These plants require good drainage, but they will tolerate almost any kind of soil. The flowers' heads yield a handsome green color when used with alum- or chrome-mordanted yarns.

Marsh marigold (*Caltha palustris*). A perennial bog or marsh plant that grows wild near ponds and streams, it can also grow in the garden if you give it plenty of water. It grows to 24 inches, with green leaves and 2-inch, butter-yellow flowers. Increase by dividing plants or by sowing seeds. The juice of the petals contains yellow coloring matter.

Mullein (*Verbascum*). These are sun-loving perennials that are somewhat weedy looking. Mullein is variously called flannel plant, candlewick plant, and velvet plant. The plants bear yellow, brownish-red, or purple flowers in July and August; the blooms contain yellow coloring matter.

Safflower or false saffron (*Carthamus tinctorius*). An annual, this member of the thistle family has spiny-leafed stems that grow to 36 inches. Seeds can be sown in place, in full sun, after frost in the spring. Give safflower a well-drained location and plenty of water; decrease watering once plants are fully established and growing. Safflower flowers contain yellow and red coloring matter.

Saffron (*Crocus sativus*). Grown from corms, these plants have grassy leaves and flaring cup-shaped flowers. Set the corms 2 to 3 inches deep in a porous soil. Yellow coloring matter is in the stigma.

Sunflower (*Helianthus annuus*). A sturdy annual that grows to 10 feet, with large flower heads in summer and fall, the plants are easily grown in any soil but need lots of sun. Sow seeds where plants are to grow in early spring. The oil obtained from pressing the seeds is a citron-yellow color.

Zinnia. This long-time favorite garden annual bears round flowers in early fall and summer. The plants like hot weather and a good water supply. Most garden zinnias belong to the species *Zinnia elegans*. The flower colors range from pink to red to orange and purple. Zinnias are easily grown from seed sown where plants are to grow in May or June; they can also be grown from nursery seedlings.

SOWING SEED

If you want lots of plants at little cost, sow seed. This always seems like a complicated procedure, but actually it is a very effortless and inexpensive way for the dyer to have the large quantity of flowers he needs.

Safflower plant *Photo by U.S. Dept. of Agricul*

Seed packets are available at nurseries and from mail-order suppliers at appropriate times of the year. Even if you are not an experienced gardener, chances are you will be successful with seeds. The odds are in your favor; it is rare not to have a few of the many seeds germinate and grow.

If you are anxious to get a head start on spring, sow seed in indoor containers. They really don't take too much space, and even the top of a refrigerator (where I keep some seed flats) will yield a harvest of tiny plants. Several plants need a long growing season to come into flower.

SEED MIXES

There are dozens of growing mediums for seeds. The most important necessity with seed mixes is a sterile growing medium so that soil-borne fungus (damping-off) does not attack small plants. You can buy packaged mixes for seeds; this is perhaps the best pro-cedure for the beginner. Packaged vermiculite is satisfactory, too. This is an expanded mica that retains moisture. Perlite is a volcanic ash and also gives good results with seed, although it does not hold moisture as long as vermiculite. Milled sphagnum moss and general soil mixes can also be used for seeds.

Containers for seed sowing range from aluminum baking tins (with holes punched in the bottom for drainage) to plastic strawberry containers to the typical 16" X 20" window-glass box called a flat. No matter which container you select, be sure it has space for about three to four inches of planting mix and that there are holes in the bottom for drainage of excess water.

To start the sowing process, fill the container with growing medium to within a quarter inch of the top. Be sure the medium is somewhat moistened. Water, let drain, and then water again; wait a few hours before sowing seed. Packet seeds are generally ready for planting, although some large seeds with thick protective coatings may have to be soaked overnight in water.

Open the seed packet and make a spout at one end by folding back the paper. Tap the seeds onto the soil. If the seeds are minute they will be in separate glassine envelopes; slit the sides and let the seed roll onto the growing medium.

As you scatter the seeds, remember to leave ample space between them because they need ventilation and room to grow. Fine seeds such as petunias and snapdragons can be merely pressed into the growing medium, but larger seeds should be set somewhat deeper. Moisten the mix thoroughly after the seeds are in place; I use a window-spray bottle from a distance of twelve inches until a mist permeates the soil. Spray gently but thoroughly so you do not dislodge fine seeds.

Some seeds need warmth for germination; others require cool conditions (this information is on the packet). If the seeds need warmth, I put them on top of the refrigerator. Cool-growing seeds in containers can be placed in the basement at about 55° F. To provide the humidity essential to germination, cover the container with a plastic sheet. Use small wooden sticks set into the sides of the container so the plastic forms a tent rather than resting directly on the growing medium. During germination the growing medium must be moderately moist at all times.

Some seeds germinate in a matter of a few days, while others require more time. When leaves are evident, remove plastic and thin out some seedlings so others don't get leggy. Remove weak ones to allow growing space for the strong ones. When the seedlings have rooted and are a few inches high, transfer them to larger containers before putting them outdoors. Some growers skip this step, but it is worth the extra time to ensure good healthy plants later.

For the second planting, use an all-purpose soil mix; keep it moist and give the plants some protection from strong sun for about five days. Then place them in bright light. When the transplanted seedlings have grown and are large enough for outdoor planting, first acclimatize them (harden them off) to their new environment. Put them in a protected outdoor area for a few days and nights before actually planting them in the garden. If the nights become chilly, return the seedlings to the house. Increase the amount of light the seedlings get by moving the boxes every few days; in about ten days seedlings should be ready for garden planting. However, do not put them in place until you are sure frost danger is over.

Soil for the new plants should be dug to a depth of about twelve inches and enriched with compost and leaf mold. When the soil bed is ready, take the plants from their containers with a small trowel, along with a portion of the soil. Water the plants before you remove them from their containers. Prepare a hole in the soil that is deep enough to accommodate the plant and its root ball. Work soil into the hole and firm it around the plant collar. Be sure there are no voids or air pockets.

The spacing of plants depends on the variety; generally space low plants six to eight inches apart, marigolds and dahlias about eighteen inches apart. After the plants are in place, water the soil thoroughly and then rewater. Water every few days until the plants are really growing.

Several perennials and annuals can be seed-sown in the open garden where they are to grow (this information is usually on the packet). Prepare the soil with some vermiculite or sphagnum, and scatter the seeds as you would for regular container plantings. Keep weeds out of the seedbed and be sure the soil is moderately moist at all times. Thin the seedlings out—remove the weak ones—when they are about three inches tall.

The time to plant seeds in the United States depends upon the regional climate.

THE SEED-SOWN GARDEN

Bloodroot *(Sanguinaria canadensis).* This perennial can be started outdoors in fall, or indoors for germination in spring. Transplanting is tricky but occasionally successful.

Butterfly weed *(Asclepias tuberosa).* A perennial wildflower that can be started indoors in spring, it needs heat and good humidity to germinate. Germination starts in about 14 days and the plants are easily transplanted outdoors.

Calendula. A group of fine annuals, these can be started indoors in March for early bloom outdoors. Calendulas need 60°F. to 65°F. for germination in about 7 days, and are best sown outdoors where they are to bloom. Space the plants 12 inches apart.

California poppy *(Eschscholtzia).* Since this is a difficult annual to start indoors and transplant, it is best to sow seed outdoors in early May. Space the plants 6 inches apart. This is a protected wild flower, so if you want flowers you must grow your own.

Calliopsis *(Coreopsis tinctoria).* Known as tickseed, this can be sown indoors in March; it germinates in about 5 days. When sown outdoors in May it germinates in about 14 days. Allow 10 to 15 inches between plants.

China aster *(Callistephus chinensis).* This annual can be sown indoors in April; outdoors, sow in late spring to germinate in about 14 days. Asters resent transplanting, so move them from indoor containers directly into the garden, weather permitting. Allow 12 inches between plants.

Chrysanthemum. This can be started indoors in March or outdoors in late spring for germination in about 20 days. Needs coolness; space the plants 15 inches apart.

Cornflower (or bachelor's button) *(Centaurea cyanus)*. Sow this perennial indoors in February for germination in about 15 days. Outdoors, cornflowers germinate in 3 weeks.

Coneflower *(Rudbeckia)*. Coneflower is best started outdoors and thinned as needed; germination in about a month.

Dahlia (treated as annuals). These are actually bulbs, but some can be easily grown from seed. You can start them indoors in March and they will germinate in about 5 days. Outdoors, sow seeds later in the year (May). Space the plants 12 to 18 inches apart, depending on the variety.

Day lily *(Hemerocallis)*. This perennial can be started indoors in March for germination in about 15 days, or in a seedbed outdoors in about 20 days. Space the plants 20 inches apart.

Helenium. A perennial; start the seeds indoors in March for germination in about 7 days; outdoor germination takes about 15 days. Space the plants 10 to 18 inches apart.

Hollyhock *(Althaea rosea)*. An annual, hollyhock can be started indoors, but it is better to sow the seeds in late spring in the garden where they are to grow. Germination occurs in about 15 days. Space the plants 10 to 16 inches apart.

Lupine *(Lupinus)*. These annual seeds germinate best in coolness (about 60°F.) and should be started in late spring in the garden. They germinate in about 3 weeks. Space 6 to 10 inches apart.

Chrysanthemum
chrysanthemum

Delphinium ajacis
larkspur

Asclepias tuberosa
butterfly weed

Prunus serotina
wild cherry

Rumex obtusifolius
dock

Cotinus coggygr
smoke-tree

Marigold (*Tagetes*). These favorite annuals are simple to grow. Sown outdoors in May, germination occurs in about 15 days. The space needed between plants depends on the variety. All plants need full sun.

Princess feather (*Polygonum*). Seeds of this annual can be started indoors in March or in the garden in May; they will germinate in about 3 weeks. Space the plants 16 to 20 inches apart.

Sunflower (*Helianthus annuus*). These annuals need warmth to germinate. Generally, growth starts in 5 to 10 days. It is best to sow the seed outdoors. Plant in early May.

Zinnia (annual). Zinnia seed can be started indoors in late March for outdoor planting in mid-May, but direct outdoor planting produces better plants. There are many varieties; space the plants according to the variety. Zinnias, whether red, yellow, or purple, yield a yellow dye.

SHRUBS

The leaves and twigs of many shrubs yield lovely dyes, and using them will not harm the plants; in fact, many shrubs benefit from pruning because it promotes better growth. With good culture shrubs will grow from year to year into handsome garden specimens and furnish good dye material.

Many shrubs are more astringent in their requirements than garden flowers, but if you start with good soil and provide adequate drainage, most shrubs will be capable performers.

Shrubs are sold in containers, balled and burlapped, or bare root (without burlap). The deciduous shrubs (they lose their foliage in winter) are available at their dormant season, bare root, and are ready for planting in spring. Broad- and narrow-leaved evergreens, such as camellias and rhododendrons, are sold in containers or balled and burlapped because they are never without leaves. Be sure to inspect the root ball; if it is very dried out, do not buy the shrub, since it will be difficult to start into growth.

If you cannot plant shrubs immediately, keep the roots moist. Put bare-root plants into a tub of water, and moisten burlapped ones until you can get them into the ground.

HOW TO PLANT SHRUBS

Make large and deep holes for shrubs so the roots can be spread out when they are put into the ground. Don't just set them in place; spread out the roots with your hands. Break up the soil in the bottom of the hole and add some topsoil, but do not bury too much of the plant's trunk below the ground. Set the bushes so the soil level is almost the same as it was at the nursery.

Do not plant shrubs closely; give them room to grow. Generally, a ten- to twelve-foot spacing is adequate for most varieties.

After you condition the soil and dig the hole, put in a mound of soil and center the plant; add soil halfway to the top of the hole and soak thoroughly. Wait a few minutes, then refill the hole with soil and soak again thoroughly.

LIST OF SHRUBS

American barberry (*Berberis vulgaris*). A deciduous shrub that grows to about 8 feet, with blue flowers in early May, the plant can sur-

opulus nigra 'Italica'
lombardy popular

Rudbeckia trilobia
coneflower

Arundinaria
cane

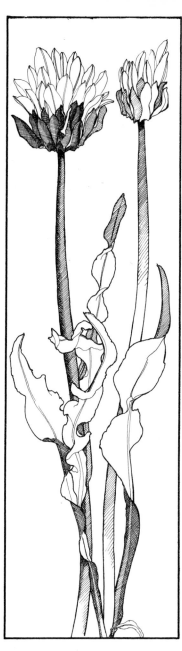

Rubus
blackberry

Helianthus
sunflower

Sambucus nigra
elderberry

vive various climates and soil conditions and still succeed. This shrub can be easily pruned when it gets too high. The roots, leaves, and stems are used for dyes. The chief constituent of barberry bark is berberine, a yellow crystalline alkaloid. The leaves are full of tannin, which produces an ash-colored dye.

Bayberry (*Myrica pensylvanica*). This is a deciduous or partly evergreen shrub with dense compact growth to 9 feet. The leaves are 4 inches long, narrow and glossy green, and dotted with resin glands. The plants tolerate poor, sandy soils but need sun. Water heavily in growth. The leaves are used for dyes, although the bark and stem contain a red coloring substance as well.

Blackberry (*Rubus*). Trailing, stiff, and upright, blackberries come in many varieties. Basically they need a rich soil, full sun, and ample water throughout the growing season. Flowering and fruiting takes place the second year. The leaves, twigs, and shoots are used in dyes; the roots and leaves contain tannin.

Camellia. These evergreen shrubs are favored throughout the country and include 3,000 named varieties. There is a wide range of color, size, and form. Camellias must have a well-drained rich soil, a somewhat shady place, and ample water (but not too much or the roots will become soggy). Feed the plants with a commercial acid food after they bloom. If necessary, camellias can be pruned after bloom when dead or weak wood is removed. *Camellia japonica* is *the* camellia, and is available in hundreds of varieties. *C. sasanqua* produces slightly smaller flowers and also has many hybrids. For dyeing you will need about six medium-sized shrubs growing through the year. The leaves are used for dyes.

Prunus persica
peach

Urtica dioica
nettle

Hypericum
St. John's wort

Common sage (*Salvia officinalis*). This is a shrub that grows to 12 inches, with white, woolly stems and purple, blue, or white flowers. The chief constituent of sage is a yellow or yellowish-green volatile oil.

Dyer's-broom (*Genista tinctoria*). A deciduous or almost leafless shrub, dyer's-broom grows to 36 inches, with slender shoots. The leaves are oval, smooth, or hairy. The flowers are in terminal racemes in June to late summer. The plants need a well-drained, somewhat light soil and a sunny place. Water moderately. The flowers are used for dyes, but all parts of the plant yield a yellow dye.

Elder (*Sambucus*). These deciduous shrubs have creamy white, fragrant flowers followed by purple-black berries. Elders are generally rampant and fast growing, but they can be kept in bounds by pruning. They need a rich, well-drained soil kept moderately moist. The bark yields black, the leaves give a green color when used, and the berries produce a blue or purple dye.

Grape holly (*Mahonia aquifolium*). These evergreen shrubs are related to barberry and have leaves that are divided into leaflets. The flowers are yellow, followed by blue-black, berrylike fruits. The plants are easily grown in almost any exposure and tolerate any conditions. When finely chopped the root is used for dyes. These plants contain berberine, a yellow alkaloid.

Heather (*Calluna*). This is the true Scotch heather, which has narrow, needlelike leaves densely set on branches and bell-shaped tubular flowers. There are many varieties and forms. The plants need a peaty, well-drained soil that is slightly acid. Heather can be sheared back after bloom to encourage fresh growth. The leaves and stems are used for dyeing.

Mountain laurel (*Kalmia latifolia*). These evergreen shrubs are related to rhododendrons and are generally slow growing to 8 feet, with glossy, leathery, oval leaves to 5 inches in length, dark green on top and yellowish-green underneath. Pale pink flowers are produced in May or June. Mountain laurel needs a moist atmosphere, partial shade, regular waterings, and a somewhat acid soil. The leaves, which contain tannic acid, are used for dyes.

New Jersey tea (*Ceanothus americanus*). This is a deciduous shrub that grows to 48 inches and has pointed, three-veined, toothed dull green leaves. Whitish blooms appear from June to August. The plants require a somewhat sandy soil and little water. The roots and leaves contain the dye matter.

Privet (*Ligustrum vulgare*). This is the common privet, a deciduous shrub with glossy, light green leaves. Clusters of black fruit appear on unpruned plants. Most privets grow easily in some sun or in shade and in almost any soil. They require buckets of water and are frequently used as hedges; the pruned parts—twigs and leaves— make excellent dyes.

Rhododendron. These are popular evergreen or deciduous shrubs with nearly 1,000 species and 10,000 varieties. The plants have leathery leaves and rounded clusters of white, pink, red, or purple blossoms. To grow rhododendrons successfully, give them an acid soil, a constant moisture supply at the roots, and excellent drainage and air movement. The soil must be rich with leaf mold and humus. Plant rhododendrons in deep holes and never bury the stems. The

Tagetes
marigolds

Juglans nigra
black walnut

Zinnia
zinnia

ideal location for rhododendrons is in the shade of trees or near a wall where they will be protected from wind and sun but will still receive bright light. There are innumerable varieties; choice depends on personal color tastes. The plants are easy to grow in large containers; indeed, they seem ideally suited to container growing. The leaves are used for dyeing.

Scotch broom (*Cytisus scoparius*). These are deciduous shrubs with bright yellow flowers in May or June. The plants grow easily in almost any soil. All parts of the plant are used for dyes. Broom contains scoparin, which appears in pale yellow crystals that are soluble in hot water.

Smoke tree (*Cotinus coggygria*). A fine shrublike tree with roundish leaves that are bluish green in summer and turn yellow to orange-red in the fall. The tree has loose clusters of greenish blossoms. Both the root and stem yield a yellow, almost orange, dye. The wood from this tree is akin to fustic.

Sumac (*Rhus*). These are evergreen or deciduous trees or shrubs. The deciduous types are hardy anywhere and grow in almost any soil. The species used for dyeing is generally *Rhus glabra,* which has rather narrow, deep green leaves that turn scarlet in the fall. Greenish flowers are followed by scarlet fruits that last on bare branches into winter. Sumac is easily grown in any soil with moderate moisture and some sun. The plant contains a yellow coloring matter.

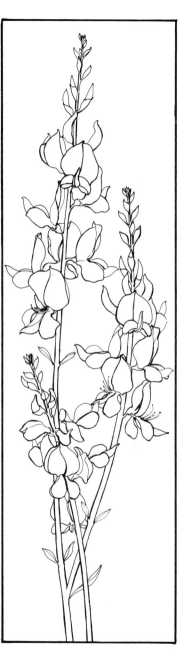

Clematis
clematis

Cytisus scoparius
scotch broom

Hemerocallis
daylily

Quercus
oak leaves

Anthemis tinctoria
golden marguerite

Fagus sylvatica
beech

onvolvulus (Ipomoea)
orning glory or bindweed

Ligustrum vulgare
privet

Ceanothus americanus
New Jersey tea

8
Dye
Recipes

The recipes that end this book should be the starting point for the reader to create his own colors from plants. While I have tested these recipes, any person who follows them may create a shade of color that is different from anyone else's because of the variable conditions involved in plant dyes.

Further, the names I have given colors are arbitrary; what may appear yellow-brown or brown-green to me may appear different to you. Refer to the color chart (where most of the colors from the recipes are shown) for true identification.

The colorfastness of certain plant materials may vary depending upon exposure to light and washing.

NOTES ON RECIPES

All these recipes are based on 1 pound of wool (dry weight.)

All dyestuffs are boiled in enough water to cover.

It takes about 30 minutes to bring solutions in all recipes to 200°F.

ACACIA PODS

Soak 1 pound of acacia pods overnight; next day boil for about 1½ hours. Strain dye liquid into pot and add cold water to make a 4- to 4½-gallon solution. Let cool. Add premordanted yarn and bring solution to 200°F.; simmer for about 1 hour. Let yarn cool in dye bath. Remove yarn and rinse.

Resulting colors with mordants:
Alum: Gray-brown
Chrome: Yellow-brown
Copper: Cocoa-brown
Tin: Beige

BLACKBERRY SHOOTS (saddened)

Twigs: 2½ pounds
Iron: ¼ ounce
Cream of tartar: ½ ounce
Cold water

Boil twigs and leaves for 1 to 2 hours. Strain dye liquid into pot and add cold water to make a 4- to 4½-gallon solution. Let cool. Add premordanted yarn and bring solution to 200°F.; simmer 45 minutes. Remove yarn. Dissolve iron and cream of tartar in small amount of water; add to dye bath. Return yarn to dye bath and cook 10 minutes. Let yarn cool in dye bath. Remove yarn and rinse.

The last 10 minutes of saddening with iron can be omitted to get somewhat brighter colors.

Resulting colors with mordants:
Alum: Black
Chrome: Deep charcoal gray
Copper: Black
Tin: Dark ocher

BLACK WALNUT HULLS

Soak 6-8 crushed walnut hulls overnight. Next day, boil for 20 minutes. Strain dye liquid into pot and add cold water to make a 4- to 4½-gallon solution. Let cool. Add premordanted yarn and bring solution to 200°F.; simmer for 1 hour. Let yarn cool in dye bath. Remove yarn and rinse.

Resulting colors with mordants:
  Alum: Light brown
  Chrome: Rust brown
  Copper: Dull brown
  Tin: Bright brown

BLACK WALNUT LEAVES

Boil 2½ pounds of leaves for about 1½ hours. Strain dye liquid into pot and add cold water to make a 4- to 4½-gallon solution. Let cool. Add premordanted yarn and bring solution to 200°F.; simmer for about 1 hour. Let yarn cool in dye bath. Remove yarn and rinse.

Resulting colors with mordants:
  Alum: Tobacco gold
  Chrome: Brown-gold
  Copper: Cinnamon brown
  Tin: Gold-brown

BOUGAINVILLEA

Boil 1 pound of flower bracts for about 2½ hours. Strain dye liquid into pot and add cold water to make a 4- to 4½-gallon solution. Let cool. Add premordanted yarn and bring solution to 200°F.; simmer for about 1 hour. Let yarn cool in dye bath. Remove yarn and rinse.

Resulting colors with mordants:
  Alum: Beige
  Chrome: Golden-brown
  Tin: Bright gold-brown

COFFEE

Boil 1¾ pounds of coffee for 20 minutes. Strain dye liquid into pot and add cold water to make a 4- to 4½-gallon solution. Let cool. Add premordanted yarn and bring solution to 200°F.; simmer 1 hour. Let yarn cool in dye bath. Remove yarn and rinse.

Resulting color with mordant:
Chrome: Brown-yellow

DOCK

Boil 1½ to 2 pounds of dock tops for about 30 minutes. Strain dye liquid into pot and add cool water to make a 4-gallon solution. Let cool. Add premordanted yarn and bring solution to 200°F.; simmer 1 hour. Let yarn cool in dye bath. Remove yarn and rinse.

Resulting color with mordant:
Alum: Brown-yellow

EUCALYPTUS BARK

Soak ¾ to 1 pound of bark overnight. Next day, grind bark and boil for about 30 minutes. Strain dye liquid into pot and add cold water to make a 4-gallon solution. Let cool. Add premordanted yarn and bring solution to 200°F.; simmer for about 1 hour. Let yarn cool in dye bath. Remove yarn and rinse.

Resulting colors with mordants:
  Alum: Beige
  Chrome: Beige-gold
  Copper: Earthy tan
  Tin: Coffee

FENNEL

Boil 2 pounds of early-growth shoots for 1 to 2 hours. Strain dye liquid into pot and add cold water to make a 4-gallon solution. Let cool. Add premordanted yarn and bring to 200°F.; simmer 1 hour. Let yarn cool in dye bath. Remove yarn and rinse.

Resulting colors with mordants:
  Alum: Light chrome-yellow
  Chrome: Yellow
  Copper: Orange-yellow
  Tin: Bright yellow

FLOWERING PLUM LEAVES

Boil 2 pounds of young, red leaves for 1 hour. Strain dye liquid into pot and add cold water to make a 4- to 4½-gallon solution. Let cool. Add premordanted yarn and bring solution to 200°F.; simmer 1 hour. Let yarn cool in dye bath. Remove yarn and rinse.

Resulting colors with mordants:
  Alum: Fern green
  Chrome: Fern green
  Copper: Gray-khaki
  Tin: Khaki

GOLDEN POPPY

Boil 1 pound of poppy flowers for 1 to 2 hours. Strain dye liquid into pot and add cool water to make a 4- to 4½-gallon solution. Let cool. Add premordanted yarn and bring solution to 200°F.; simmer 1 hour. Let yarn cool in dye bath. Remove yarn and rinse.

Resulting color with mordant:
  Tin: Gold

HEATHER

Boil 1 pound of heather for about 1 hour. Strain dye liquid into pot and add cool water to make a 4-gallon solution. Let cool. Add premordanted yarn and bring solution to 200°F.; simmer about 1½ hours. Let yarn cool in dye bath. Remove yarn and rinse.

Resulting color with mordant:
  Alum: Greenish-yellow

HORSETAIL

Boil 2 pounds of horsetail shoots for 1 to 2 hours. Strain dye liquid into pot and add cool water to make a 4- to 4½-gallon solution. Let cool. Add premordanted yarn and bring solution to 200°F.; simmer for about 1 hour. Let yarn cool in dye bath. Remove yarn and rinse.

Resulting colors with mordants:
  Alum: Pink-tan
  Chrome: Sand
  Copper: Tan
  Tin: Camel tan

LICHEN (yellow)

Soak 1 pound of lichen overnight. Next day, boil for 1 hour. Strain dye liquid into pot and add cold water to make a 4- to 4½-gallon solution. Let cool. Add premordanted wool and bring solution to 200°F.; simmer for 1 hour. Let yarn cool in dye bath. Remove yarn and rinse.

Resulting color with mordant:
  Alum: Orange-yellow

LICHEN WITH INDIGO OVERDYE

Boil 1 pound of lichen for 20 minutes. Strain dye liquid into pot and add cold water to make a 4- to 4½-gallon solution. Let cool. Add unmordanted yarn and bring solution to 200°F.; simmer 1 hour. Dip yarn into medium indigo dye bath. Remove yarn and air for 15 minutes.

Resulting color with no mordant: Blue-green

LOGWOOD CHIPS

Soak 1½ ounces of chips overnight. Next day, boil for about 30 minutes. Strain dye liquid into pot and add cool water to make a 4- to 4½-gallon solution. Let cool. Add premordanted yarn and bring solution to 200°F.; simmer 1 hour. Let yarn cool in dye bath. Remove yarn and rinse.

Resulting colors with mordants:
  Alum: Lavender-gray
  Chrome: Blue-gray
  Copper: Lavender-gray
  Tin: Grape-violet

LOMBARDY POPLAR LEAVES

Boil 1½ pounds of leaves for about 1½ hours. Strain dye liquid into pot and add cold water to make a 4- to 4½-gallon solution. Let cool. Add premordanted yarn and bring solution to 200°F.; simmer for about 1 hour. Let yarn cool in dye bath. Remove yarn and rinse.

Resulting colors with mordants:
  Alum: Gray-green
  Chrome: Lime green
  Tin: Lime green

LUPINE FLOWERS (purple)

Boil 1 pound of flowers for about 30 minutes. Strain dye liquid into pot and add cold water to make a 4- to 4½-gallon solution. Let cool. Add premordanted yarn and bring solution to 200°F.; simmer 1 hour. Let yarn cool in dye bath. Remove yarn and rinse.

Resulting colors with mordants:
  Alum: Lime green
  Chrome: Willow green
  Copper: Celadon green
  Tin: Grass green

PRIVET BERRIES

Pit and crush 1 pound of berries. Boil for 20 to 30 minutes. Strain dye liquid into pot and add cold water to make a 4- to 4½-gallon solution. Let cool. Add premordanted yarn and bring solution to 200°F.; simmer 1 hour. Let yarn cool in dye bath. Remove yarn and rinse.

Resulting colors with mordants:
  Alum: Blue-gray
  Chrome: Green-gray

PRIVET LEAVES

Boil 2½ pounds of privet leaves for 1 hour. Strain dye liquid into pot and add cool water to make a 4- to 4½-gallon solution. Let cool. Add premordanted yarn and bring solution to 200°F.; simmer 1 hour. Let yarn cool in dye bath. Remove yarn and rinse.

Resulting colors with mordants:
  Alum: Yellow-green
  Chrome: Chartreuse green

RED ONION SKINS

Soak 1 pound of skins and then boil until most of the skins have lost their color. Strain dye liquid into pot and add cold water to make a 4-gallon solution. Let cool. Add premordanted yarn and bring to 200°F.; simmer 1 hour. Let yarn cool in dye bath. Remove yarn and rinse.

    You will generally get rusty-red colors but if you

rinse the yarn in clear ammonia (2 tablespoons to 3 or 4 gallons of water), you will get green.

Resulting colors with mordants:
  Alum: Red-brown
  Chrome: Red-brown
  Copper: Orange-brown
  Tin: Deep red-brown

RHODODENDRON LEAVES

Boil 2 pounds of leaves for about 1 to 2 hours. Strain dye liquid into pot and add cold water to make a 4- to 4½-gallon solution. Let cool. Add premordanted yarn and bring solution to 200°F.; simmer for about 1 hour. Let yarn cool in dye bath. Remove yarn and rinse.

Resulting colors with mordants:
  Alum: Tan
  Chrome: Dark tan
  Copper: Brown
  Tin: Bright tan

STAG'S HORN MOSS

Soak 1 pound of moss overnight. Next day, boil for 1 hour. Strain dye liquid into pot and add cold water to make a 4- to 4½-gallon solution. Let cool. Add premordanted yarn and bring solution to 200°F.; simmer for 1 hour. Let yarn cool in dye bath. Remove yarn and rinse.

Resulting color with mordant:
  Alum: Yellow

SAGE

Boil 2 pounds of sage tips 1 to 2 hours. Strain dye liquid into pot and add cold water to make a 4-gallon solution. Let cool. Add premordanted yarn and bring solution to 200° F.; simmer 1 hour. Let yarn cool in dye bath. Remove yarn and rinse.

Resulting colors with mordants:
Alum: Yellow ocher
Chrome: Yellow ocher
Copper: Yellow ocher
Tin: Lemon yellow

SILVER DOLLAR EUCALYPTUS (tin bloomed)

Boil 2 pounds of fresh leaves for 1 hour. Strain dye liquid into pot and add cold water to make a 4- to 4½-gallon solution. Let cool. Add premordanted yarn and bring solution to 200° F.; simmer 1 hour. Let yarn cool in dye bath. Remove yarn and rinse.

Resulting colors with mordants:
Alum: Yellow-orange
Chrome: Orange-brown
Copper: Bright brown

YELLOW ONION SKINS

Soak 1 pound of skins and then boil until most of the skins have lost their color. Strain dye liquid into pot and add cold water to make a 4-gallon solution. Let cool. Add premordanted yarn and bring to 200° F.; simmer 1 hour. Let yarn cool in dye bath. Remove yarn and rinse.

Resulting colors with mordants:
  Alum: Dull yellow
  Chrome: Yellow
  Copper: Gold-yellow
  Tin: Bright gold-yellow

Color Charts

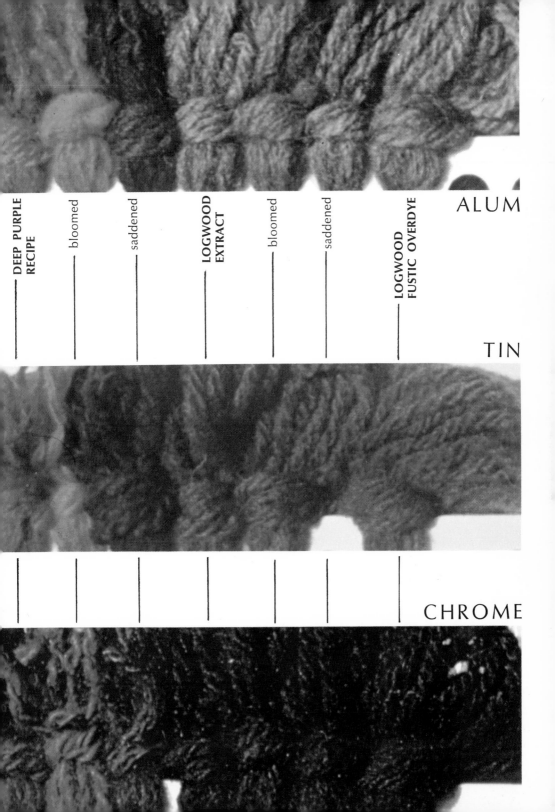

ALUM

| | DEEP PURPLE RECIPE | bloomed | saddened | LOGWOOD EXTRACT | bloomed | saddened | LOGWOOD FUSTIC OVERDYE |

TIN

CHROME

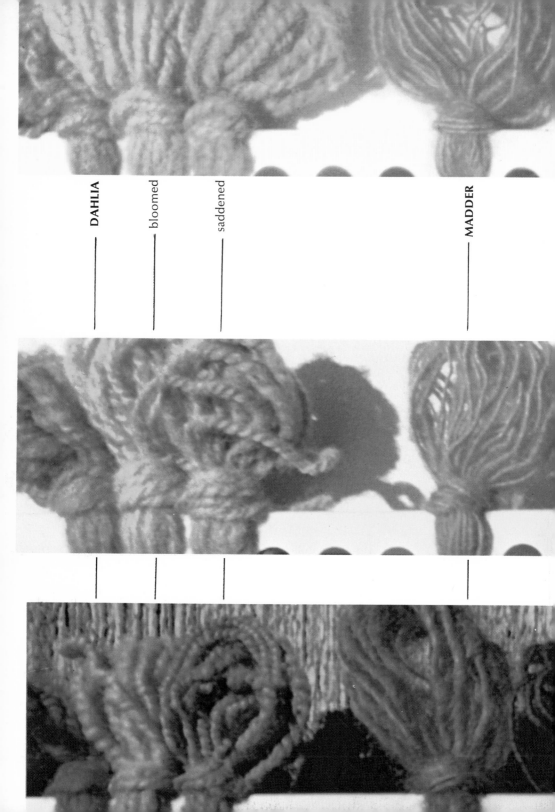

DAHLIA

bloomed

saddened

MADDER

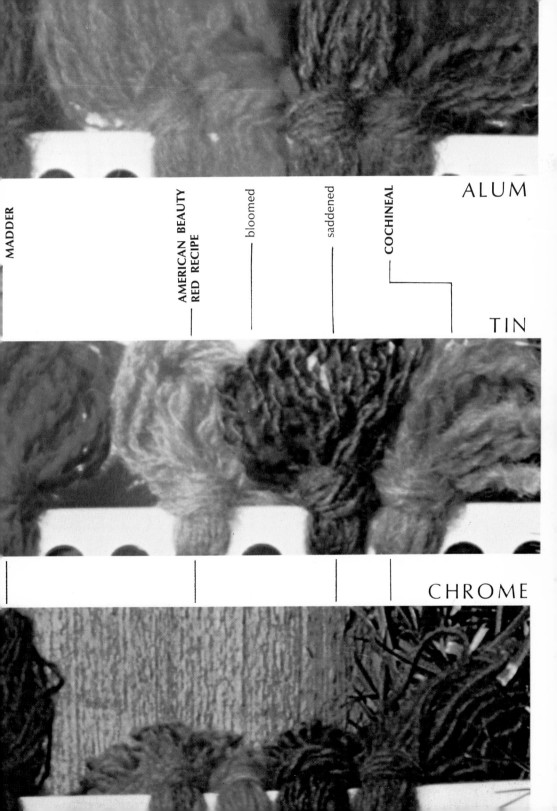

ALUM

MADDER

AMERICAN BEAUTY
RED RECIPE

— bloomed

— saddened

COCHINEAL

TIN

CHROME

WASH BLUE
INDIGO OVERDYE

PEACH
Alum

Alum
bloomed

Tin
saddened

Chrome

Chrome
bloomed

WILLOW
Alum

Chrome

Chrome
bloomed

SCOTCH BROOM
Alum
bloomed

Tin

Chrome
bloomed

LIGHT BLUE
INDIGO OVERDYE

PEACH
Tin

Chrome
bloomed

Chrome

Alum

Alum
bloomed

WILLOW
Alum

Alum
bloomed

Alum
saddened

Tin
saddened

Chrome

Chrome
saddened

SCOTCH
BROOM
Alum

Tin

Chrome

EUCALYPTUS
PODS ALUM

ECUALYPTUS
BARK ALUM

Tin

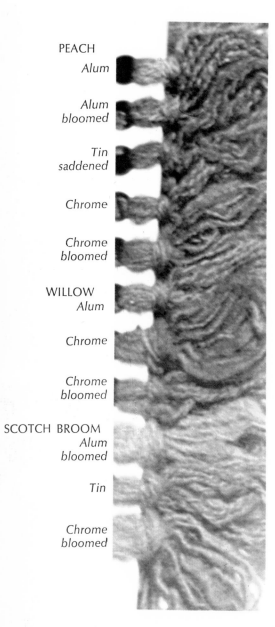

MEDIUM BLUE
INDIGO OVERDYE

PEACH
Alum
saddened

Tin

WILLOW
Alum

Alum
bloomed

Alum
saddened

Chrome

Chrome
bloomed

SCOTCH BROOM
Alum
bloomed

Alum
saddened

Tin

Chrome

Chrome
bloomed

WALNUT

PEACH
Alum

Alum
bloomed

Tin
saddened

Chrome

Chrome
bloomed

WILLOW
Alum

Chrome

Chrome
bloomed

SCOTCH BROOM
Alum
bloomed

Tin

Chrome
bloomed

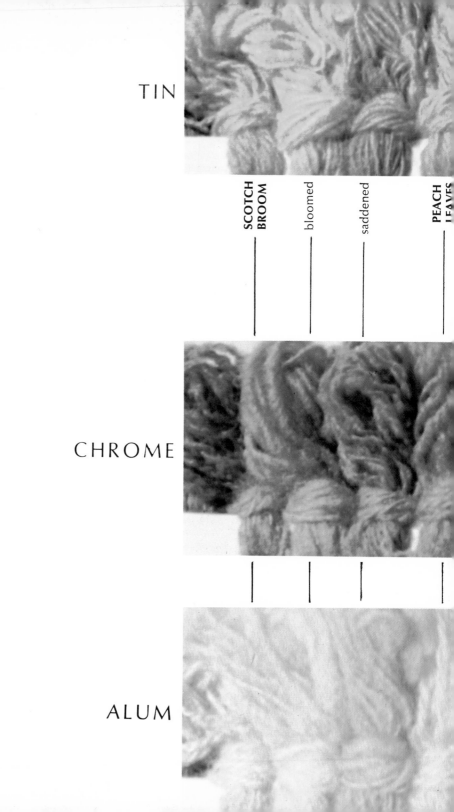

TIN

SCOTCH BROOM

bloomed

saddened

PEACH LEAVES

CHROME

ALUM

bloomed

saddened

FUSTIC EXTRACT

bloomed

saddened

PRIVET LEAVES

bloomed

saddened

ALMOND LEAVES

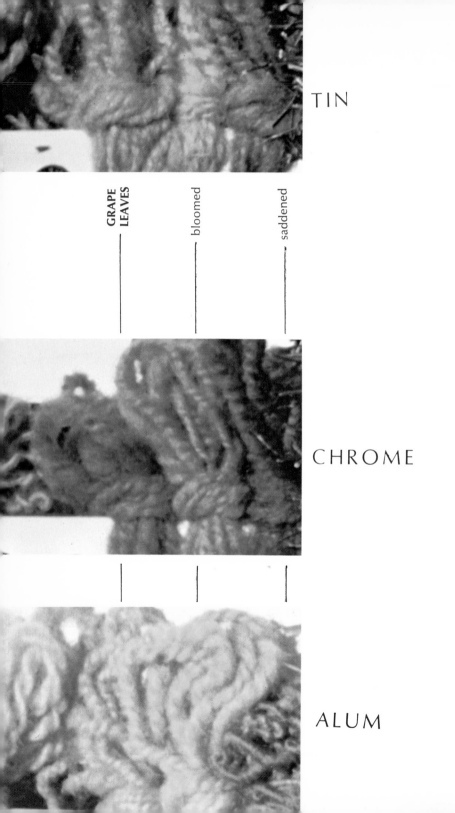

TIN

**GRAPE
LEAVES**

bloomed

saddened

CHROME

ALUM

Appendix

INFORMATION ON SUPPLIES

Plant materials not native to this country—madder, logwood, fustic, and so forth—can be purchased from mail order suppliers. However, some cities do have specialty botanical or herb shops that stock these dye substances. And recently many yarn shops have started to stock some of these dyes. Check the yellow pages of your local phone book or write the following suppliers:

Comak Chemicals Ltd.
Swinton Works
Moon Street
London NI
England

C.D. Fitz Harding-Bailey
15 Dutton Street
Bankstown, NSW 2200
Australia

Kem Chemical Co.
545 S. Fulton Street
Mt. Vernon, N.Y. 10550

Kiehl Pharmacy
109 Third Avenue
New York, N.Y. 10003

Dominion Herb Distributors
61 St. Catherine Street West
Montreal, Quebec, Canada

Nature's Herb Company
281 Ellis Street
San Francisco, Calif. 94102

Sheep Village
352 Miller Avenue
Mill Valley, Calif. 94941

Some of the chemicals for mordants can be found at drug stores or from the above suppliers. Local chemical companies (in yellow pages of phone book) will generally not sell to the public but they can direct you to dealers for chemicals.

Yarns are available at most yarn stores or from weaving supply companies.

Wm. Condon & Sons, Ltd.
Charlottetown
P.E. Island, Canada

Davidson's Old Mill Yarn
Box 115
Eaton Rapids, Mich. 48827

Dharma Trading Co.
1952 University Avenue
P.O. Box 1288
Berkeley, Calif. 94701

Folklorico
P.O. Box 625
Palo Alto, Calif. 94202

Jamiesons Knitwear
115 Commercial Street
Lerwick, Shetland Isles
Scotland

Kalevala Koru
Fredrikinkatu 41C
Helsinki 12, Finland

Meg Swanson
Box 57
Trumansburg, N.Y. 14886

New York Yarn Center
866 Avenue of the Americas
New York, N.Y. 10001

The Yarn Depot, Inc.
545 Sutter Street
San Francisco, Calif. 94102

Yarn Primitives
P.O. Box 1013
Weston, Conn. 06880

SOURCES FOR PLANTS

Local garden centers furnish many of the plants for dyes—marigolds, chrysanthemums, and so forth. Native plants such as bloodroot and butterfly weed, and seed, can be found at mail order suppliers that follow:

Clyde Robin
P.O. Box 2091
Castro Valley, Calif. 94546

Leslie's Wildflower Nursery
30 Summer Street
Methuen, Mass. 01844

Lamb's Nurseries
E. 101 Sharp Avenue
Spokane, Wash. 99202

Midwest Wildflowers
Box 664B
Rockton, Ill. 61072

Mail order plant suppliers that carry dye plants such as false indigo, alkanet, turmeric, safflower and other plants:

Nichol's Garden Nursery
1190 N. Pacific Highway
Albany, Oregon 97321

Merry Gardens
Camden, Maine 04843

BOOKS OF INTEREST

Natural Dyes and Home Dyeing, Rita J. Adrosko, Dover Publications, Inc. New York, 1971. (Originally published in 1968 as United States National Museum Bulletin 281: *Natural Dyes in the United States,* Smithsonian Institution Press, publisher of original edition.)

Dye Plants and Dyeing, a Handbook, Brooklyn Botanic Gardens.

Vegetable Dyeing, Alma Lesch, Watson Guptill, New York, 1970.

A History of Dyed Textiles, Stuart Robinson, M.I.T. Press, Cambridge Mass. (First published in Great Britain by Studio Vista Limited, 1969.)

Other books on plant dyes and books for weavers and craftsmen are available from:

Craft and Hobby Book Service
P.O. Box 626
Pacific Grove, Calif. 93950

Index

Acacia *(Acacia baileyana)*, 50
Acacia catechu, 74
Acacia pods (recipe), 115
African marigold *(Tagetes erecta)*, 85-86
Alder tree *(Alnus)*, 23, 47, 50
Alectoria sarmentosa, 59
Alizarin, 67
Alkalinity, water, 30
Alkanet *(Alkanna tinctoria)*, 85
Alnus glutinosa, 50
Alum (aluminum potassium sulfate), 25, 32-34
American barberry *(Berberis vulgaris)*, 102-105
American smoke tree *(Cotinus coggygria)*, 70-71, 110
Annuals and perennials, 84-92
 list of, 85-92
 planting and watering, 84-85
 seed mixes, 94-96
 seed-sown garden, 97-101
 soil bed for, 84
 sowing process, 92-96
Apple bark *(Malus)*, 54
Areca catechu, 74

Bayberry *(Myrica pensylvanica)*, 105
Beets, 56
Berries, picking, 47
Biennials, 84, 90
Birch tree *(Betula)*, 23, 50
Black dyed color, 64
Black oak *(Q. velutina)*, 52
Black walnut *(J. nigra)*, 49, 54

Black walnut hulls, 116-117
Blackberry *(Rubus)*, 46, 105
Blackberry shoots (saddened), 116
Blackberry twigs, 23
Bloodroot *(Sanguinaria canadensis)*, 86, 97
Blooming (brightening) a color, 62
Blue, color combinations, 80-81
Bougainvillea, 44, 117
Bracken *(Pteridium aquilinum)*, 55
Broom sedge *(Andropogon virginicus)*, 55
Brown dyed color, 63, 74
Butternut *(Juglans cinerea)*, 23, 54
Butterfly weed *(Asclepias tuberosa)*, 86, 97

Calendula (annuals), 97
Calgon (water softener), 30
California poppy *(Eschscholtzia)*, 97
Calliopsis *(Coreopsis tinctoria)*, 86, 97
Camellia, 105
Canadian hemlock *(T. canadensis)*, 52
Cane *(Arundinaria macrosperma)*, 55
Canoe birch *(B. papyrifera)*, 50
Cetraria glauca, 59
Chamomile *(Anthemis nobilis)*, 86
China aster *(Callistephus chinensis)*, 89, 97
Chrome (potassium dichromate), 25, 34-36
Chrysanthemum, 89, 98
Cochineal, 75-76
Coffee (dye recipe), 118
Coffee beans, 56

Color, 77-82
  basics, 79-80
  blooming (brightening), 62
  combinations, 80-81
  contrasting side by side, 82
  in compositions, 81-82
  hues, 79
  intensity, or saturation, 79-80
  natural beauty of, 21-25
  notes on, 63-64
  shade darkness, 80
  tint, 80
  top-dyeing for, 65
  value, or tone, 79
Colorfastness, 42, 67, 71, 114
  testing for, 64
Commercial woods, 66-76
Common sage (Salvia officinalis), 107
Coneflower (Rudbeckia), 89, 98
Copper sulfate (blue vitriol), 32, 36
Cornflower (bachelor's button), (Centaurea cyanus), 89, 98
Cotton and linen
  mordanting, 32, 40-41
  washing, 30
  working with, 22
Cutch (Catechu), 66, 74

Dahlia, 44, 46, 89-90, 96, 98
Dandelion (Taraxacum officinale), 55
Day lily (Hemerocallis), 90, 98
Dock (Rumex obtusifolius), 46, 55, 118
Dried flowers, 46
Dye materials, getting, 43-59
Dye recipes, 114-127
Dyeing process, 60-65
  blooming and saddening wool, 62
  colorfastness, 64
  drying yarn, 61
  notes on dyed colors, 63-64
  steps to follow, 61

  storing dye solution, 62
  timing, 61
  top-dyeing, 65
  water temperature, 60-61
Dyer's-broom (Genista tinctoria), 107

Elder (Sambucus), 107
Equipment, dyeing, 25
Eucalyptus, 23, 52, 118-119

False saffron (Carthamus tinctorius), 92
Fennel, 119
Florist's chrysanthemum (C. morifolium), 89
Flowering dogwood (Cornus florida), 52, 54
Flowering plum leaves, 119
Flowers, 44-46
  annuals and perennials, 84-92
  biennials, 84, 90
  extracting color from, 46
  seed-sown garden, 97-102
Fustic (Morus tinctoria, or Chlorophora tinctoria), 23, 65, 66, 70-71

Gall nuts, 28
Gambier (Uncaria gambir), 74
Gardens, 83-110
Golden poppy (recipe), 120
Goldenrod (Solidago canadensis), 23, 65, 90
Grape holly (Mahonia aquifolium), 107
Grasses, list of, 55
Gray dyed color, 64
Green dyed color, 63
  color combinations, 80-81
  top-dyeing for, 65

Heather (Calluna), 107-108
Heather (recipe), 120

Helenium, 98
Hemlock *(Tsuga)*, 47, 52
Hickory *(Carya tomentosa)*, 52
Hollyhock *(Althaea rosea)*, 90, 98
Horsetail (recipe), 120
Hulls, extracting color from, 49-50

Indigo *(Indigofera tinctoria)*, 23, 64,
    66, 72-73
Iron (ferrous sulfate), 25, 32, 38-39
Ivory Flakes (detergent), 30

Larkspur *(Delphinium ajacis)*, 91
Leaves, 23
    extracting color from, 46-47
Lichen, 23-24, 28
    collecting, 56-58
    dye recipes, 122
    list of, 58-59
Lily of the valley *(Convallaria ma-
    jalis)*, 91
Logwood *(Haematoxylon campechia-
    num)*, 23, 66, 70
Logwood chips, 122
Lombardy poplar leaves *(Populus ni-
    gra* 'Italica'), 54, 123
Lupine *(Lupinus)*, 91, 98, 123

Madder *(Rubia tinctorum)*, 23, 64, 66,
    67-69
Magenta, recipe for, 75
Mail order suppliers, 138-139
Maple tree bark, 47
Marguerite *(C. frutescens)*, 23, 89
Marigold *(Tagetes)*, 44, 96, 101
Marigold American *(Tagetes erecta)*,
    85-86
Marsh marigold *(Caltha palustris)*, 91
Mockernut *(Carya tomentosa)*, 52
Mordanting yarn, 22, 32-42
    chemicals, 32-39

cotton and linen, 32, 40-41
how to start, 32
meaning of, 26
silk, 41-42
storage containers, 25
undyed yarn, 39
with and after the dye, 42
wool, 32-39
Mountain laurel *(Kalmia latifolia)*, 108
Mullein *(Verbascum)*, 19

New Jersey tea *(Ceanothus ameri-
    canus)*, 108
Nettle *(Urtica dioica)*, 55
Nonmordant dyes, 28

Oak *(Quercus)*, 52
Onion skins, 23
    dye recipes, 124-125, 127
Orange dyed color, 63
    bright orange, 76
    color combinations, 80
    recipes, 69, 76
    top-dyeing for, 65

Parmelia centrifuga (green lichen), 58
P. omphalodes (brown lichen), 58
P. saxatilis, 58
Peach *(Prunus persica)*, 52
Pecan *(Carua illinoenis)*, 52
Princess feather *(Polygonum)*, 101
Privet *(Lagustrum vulgare)*, 23, 108,
    124
Purple dyed color, 63
Pyrethrum *(Chrysanthemum coccine-
    um)*, 88

Queen Anne's lace *(Daucus carota)*,
    55
Quercitron, 52
Quercus velutina, 52

Raffia, mordanting, 32
Red bougainvillea, 44
Red dyed color, 63
    American beauty red, 75
    recipes for, 67, 75
    top-dyeing for, 64
Red oak (Q. rubra), 52
Red onion skins, 124-125
Rhododendron, 108-110, 125
Roots, collecting, 49

Saddening wool, 62
Safflower (Carthamus tinctorius), 92
Sage (recipe), 126
Saint-John's-wort (Hypericum perforatum), 55
Sassafras (Sassafras albidum), 54
Scotch broom (Cytisus scoparius), 110
Seed sowing, 92-96
    garden, 97-102
    mixes for, 94-96
Shasta daisy (C. maximum), 89
Shrinkage, avoiding, 30
Shrubs, 101-110
    how to plant, 102
    list of, 102-110
Silk, mordanting, 41-42
Smartweed (Polygonum hydropiper), 23, 46, 55
Spinach, 56
Stag's horn moss, 125
Stems, 55-56
Sumac (Rhus), 54, 110
Sunflower (Helianthus annuus), 101
Supplies, 138-140
    sources for plants, 140
Sweet birch (B. lenta), 50

Tannic acid, 23, 32, 49
Tea leaves, 56

Tin (stannous chloride), 25, 32, 38
Top-dyeing, 65
Tree barks, 23
    collecting, 47
    drying for future use, 49
    extracting color from, 47-49
Trees, list of, 50-54
Twigs, 55-56

Unbleached wool, 22

Vines, 55-56
Violet, recipe for, 70

Walnut tree bark, 23
Water softeners, 30
Weeds, 21, 22, 46
    list of, 55
White oak (Q. alba), 52
White walnut (Juglans cinerea), 54
Wild cherry (Prunus serotina), 50-52
Wild indigo (Baptisia tinctoria), 72
Wool
    mordanting, 32-39
    preparing, 28
    removing oil from, 22, 28
    saddening, 62
    washing, 30
    working with, 22
Work space, 24

Yarn, buying, 22
Yellow birch (B. lutea), 50
Yellow onion skins, 127
Yellow dyed color, 63
    bright yellow recipe, 71
    color combinations, 80-81
    top-dyeing for, 64
Yellow-orange dyed color, 63

Zinnia (annual), 101